Out Here

Out Here

poems 1989–2000

Joseph Keller McNeilly

Library of Congress Cataloguing-in-Publication Data
McNeilly, Joseph Keller.
Out Here : poems 1989-2000 / Joseph Keller McNeilly
p.   cm.
0-9661452-3-2
PS3553.A319A53 2000
811.54--dc2   00-106259

ISBN: 0-9661452-3-2

Cover Painting: 1. John Rogers Cox, American, 1915-1990. Grey and Gold, 1942. Oil on canvas, 90.8 x 125.7 cm. © The Cleveland Museum of Art, 1999, Mr. and Mrs. William H. Marlatt Fund, 1943.60

Book design by Susana Wessling
Photo of Joseph McNeilly by Tamara Wagner

Published in the United States by
Chatoyant
PO Box 832
Aptos, CA 95001
www.chatoyant.com

The Song of Bricks Falling was previously published by Quarry West.

Printed in Canada

Table of Contents

THESE DAYS

whatever you have to say, leave
the roots on, let them dangle

and the dirt

      just to make clear
      where they came from

Charles Olson

Let me be the first to admit that the naked truth about me
is to the naked truth about Salvador Dali as an old ukulele
in the attic is to a piano in a tree, and I mean a piano with
breasts.

James Thurber

We notice that no one can see us from the shore at all, no
one can help us. We're all out here you see. So we don't
drown, we beat our hands, more or less, in the water, in
the air, and splash all around us. A way of swimming? Why
can't we tell the difference? Why do we pretend it's the
swimming we learned as children?

Walter Helmut Fritz
Translated by Stuart Friebert

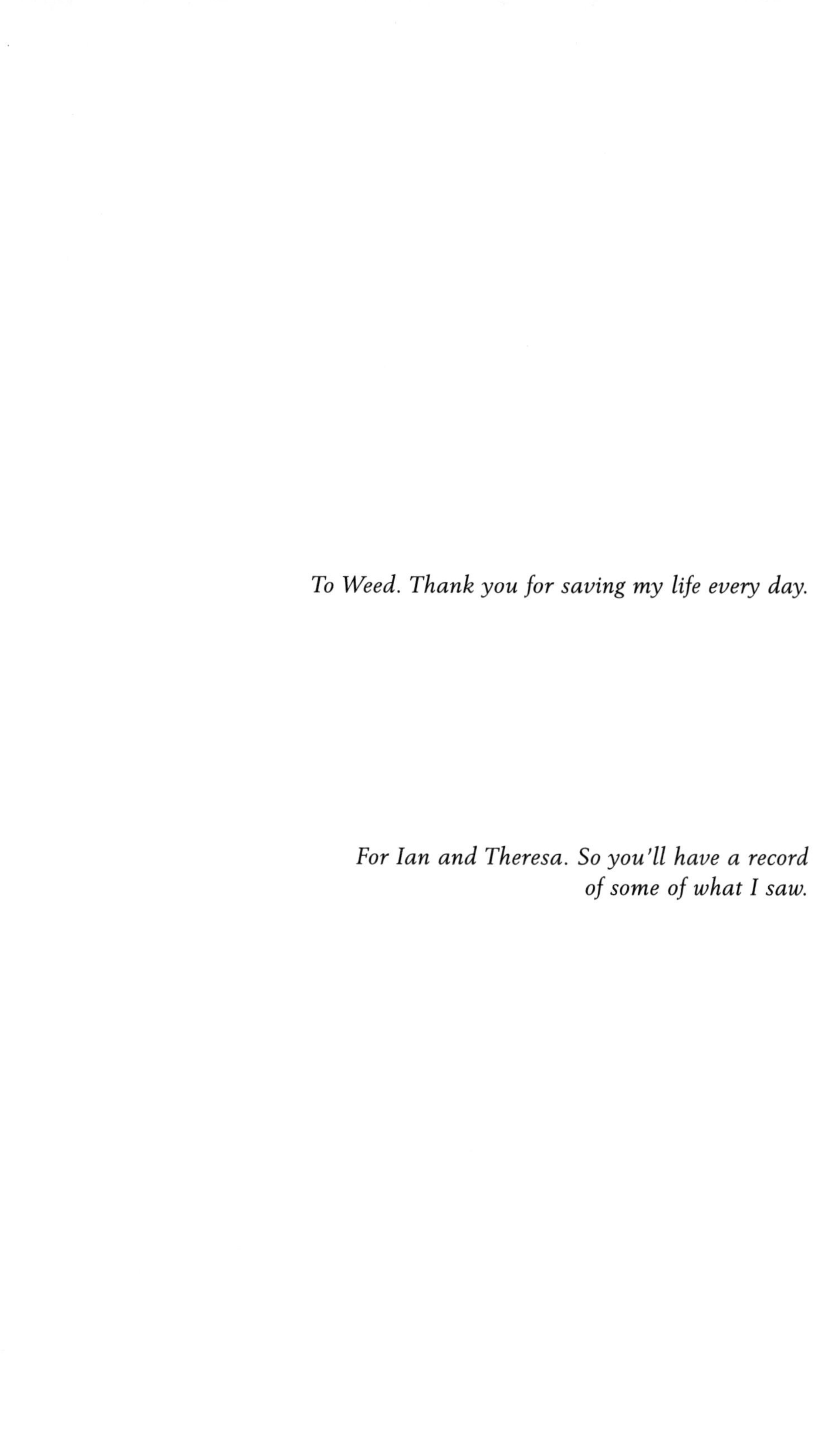

To Weed. Thank you for saving my life every day.

For Ian and Theresa. So you'll have a record of some of what I saw.

Out Here

EVERY HOUSE A DOG

Out here alone
walking this narrow, alligator-backed road
you keep a stick
always in your hand, a green stick
that will not snap
when you whip it, because
under every porch out here
there is a sorry black or brown dusty dog
waiting
for something, something slow-footed
and smelling like meat
to break its boredom, reward
its vigilance. Along this road
there are no pedigreed
or fancy-papered dogs. These
scrawny, desperate dogs are sprung
from the pound or found
abandoned in barns
or inherited from starving litters
to guard the right of their masters
to be angry and hate
for the sake of hating. Out here
anger comes first, and meanness
marks each house
with peeling paint, weeds
and crumbling stoops. There are never
flowers in these yards
and even the wildflowers seem
to stop at the property lines
as if knowing
that even accidental beauty
is not welcome here.

These dogs are trained
in the same manner

as children, through
apprenticeship, and learn in time
to mimic the stooped postures, brooding
ill humor and sullen growls
of their owners, and come
eventually
not to miss touch in any form
except from a stick, a stone
or a cuff on the muzzle.

When these dogs
spring at you
my advice is this: stand
your ground, stare
them down, spit
and show them
the stick. Wait
for them to mew, turn
and crawl again
under the porch, under
the scrub oak. Show them kindness
and you will lose a hand
or your throat. Smile at them
and they will seize you
and never let go. I know this
because I once lived
on this road
in a mean house with
a rawboned, ink-colored dog
which died, finally, starved
to death
because one day
I could no longer remember
how to feed it.

SUNDAY

At daybreak, my family
still sleeping, I walk
an isolated, stony, two-rut road
along the Russian River. A mile in
I come across (like you come across
a shoe thought lost) a peeling, slat-board building tucked away
behind a grove of gnarled oaks. It's
the Guerneville Calvary Bible Church
the fading sign above the door says, just letting out. As I pass
two warped doors creak open
and out files a terrifying line of ancient stick-skinny humanoids
   dressed
in bagging dark suits and wide ties and
pillbox hats and dresses like wallpaper wearing
wingtips and white sox and stockings with snags
and black pumps
that clatter and crack like pool balls
across the worn boards
of the porch. More women
than men, all moving it seems
with pain, slowly, without speaking, some
arm-and-arm, others
very much alone, their eyes
fixed to their feet.

I count eleven
in all
though the church has pews
for a hundred.

They slowly spill into the morning sun (which turns their
   cobweb shocks of hair blood red) and inch their way
toward the boxy old Fords and Chevys parked in the tall
   blue rattling grass. I can smell them, a dizzying stink
of tired perfumes and must and b.o.

and aftershaves smelling
like new boots.

Most
pay me no mind, but
the last, a short, chicken-boned man, nods to me
as he pulls the big doors shut and locks them
with a great brass key, me
the tourist, the vacationer. I'm
oddly unnerved
by the brittle little man, feel hollow
and uneasy that I hold nothing for this congregation
save curiosity: What plague
took their children? What
will become of the building
and the idea
when the last big shiny satin-lined box
is buried in the rocky dirt
out back, out behind
the peeling church, and Sunday
is just a day
between Saturday
and Monday?

CARRIED CHILD

Through the window
I see a young woman
carrying a child
on her hip, a daughter
perhaps two, riding her mother's bones
through the light rain
with urgency to somewhere. The woman is
nose to nose with the child, smiling
broadly, speaking
wildly to the child
about some business or other. The child
is not handsome and is
by the meanest measures
ugly
except for the smile returned
and the beautiful pink hands
holding fast
to her mother's ears.

THE SEMIOTICS OF FLOWERS

Way out here
on the meanest
of dirt roads, on the hottest
day of the year, here's this
Botero, a big, scary, bikini-clad woman
in front of the bleakest shack
on the mean road, smoking
a cigarette and drowning
a small patch of flowers
with a thick stream
from a bright green hose.

Even
at this distance, with my
bad eyes, I can see
their colored heads—*three*
red, one yellow, one
white—bobbing, set in motion
by the splashing water. These are
the only flowers for miles, an oasis
amid the acres
of bronze grasslands. There
is pride in her stance, and maybe
defiance, too: these flowers
by god
will live to see
a jar on the little table
lurking beyond
the torn screen door. There
will be beauty in her life
by god, and pity
all insects, gophers
or smirking men.

Dorothy, too, my
mother, Medea
without the guts, nursed every summer
a patch of Zinnias
out beyond the chicken house, out beyond
the meanness of her house, beyond
the reach of him. She was partial
to the red ones, and the purple.

I hauled the buckets
of chicken shit, turned
the stinking green-white putty
into the bed, while she
pushed the seeds into the mix
with a stick. Though she sang
in choir, only here
were her pipes
thrown open. At least once each planting
she'd soar into an aria
and tell me how Zinnias
were tough customers, didn't
bow down
to anything, even
a hard rain. And
when you take them finally inside
she boasted
they were loud in their brown jar
and lasted
a long time.

For eons
tending small beds of flowers
has been
the province of women. Travel
anywhere, and you will see them
in hide gloves, veils, scarves
or broad-billed hats, on their knees

or bent smartly
at the waist, their butts thrust out
at the world. So much beauty
forced outside
where it is safe
to be beautiful, brought in
a few stalks at a time
as a reminder.

FOG FOLIO

1.

Along this section of coast
the fog comes in thick, cold
and in the summer stays
all day, too long, like a shirt-tail aunt
who visits and visits
and shows no signs
of going home. You learn
in this gray part of the world
to shrug and make small talk
with auntie, even make her
a pot of tea while you wait for her
to tire and retire for a nap. You pray
that she dies in her sleep
and then miss her a little
when she does.

2.

Here
the fog is thickest
in morning. Walking
in this dense stuff of colliding hot and cold
is like swimming in the ocean
at night: there are moments
when you lose left from right
and the way to land is fuzzy
so you drown.

On such a morning
when all seems lost and lonely
a woman materializes, gathers
molecules, comes toward me
out of the fog
dressed all in bright white, and even

a white turban, a long white scarf
wound round and around
and stacked high
like a beehive
on her head. She is frightening
and impressive, like one of the Alps
and is stunning against the sand and fog
like a dollop of snow found out of
the context of winter, and what sun there is
filtering now down through the fog
makes all of this something
unearthly, holy.

Is it God
I wonder
come finally
to have that little talk with me? If so
I have questions.

3.

What's the story here
at 6:12 a.m., foggy
and cold along the tide line? It's
a puckered, skinny old naked man
kicking up his heels, leaping
into the air as best he can, clapping
his feet together
again and again, his penis
drawing impressive arcs in the fog
each time he leaps. He is muttering words
I can't make out
and now, as I close in, I see
he's smiling
and does not stop his dance
as I pass by. I say nothing
to him, leave him to it
in the fog. Perhaps this morning

he has declared himself
the happy genius of this beach, a title
I'll let him have
just for today.

4.

Holy Hieronymus, look
at this! Rolling up to me
on the high tide
are a tight-dimpled orange, a crisp
green apple and
a ripe cantaloupe. The tumbling fruit
glistens even under the hooded light
which manages to bull through
the fog. Under inspection
each piece is perfect, as if
just escaped by sea
from the market, or liberated
from someone's lunch. And as I gather
them up, who's this watching from a rock
but Fellini himself
disguised as an old whiskered seal
barking?

LOOKING DOWN

When designing gardens
Christopher Wren always sculpted
crooked, winding paths
through the hollyhock, mustard
and roses. It was essential
he thought
to slow you down, force you
to pick your way
over the stones, to look
down. Only then
maybe
you would notice the flowers
and the bugs
crawling over the blooms
and maybe
you would be pulled
out of yourself like taffy
and see. *Walking slowly*
he wrote close to death
is the true speed
of the human mind, the speed
the true eye needs. Four-horse carriages
and trains
would be our ruin
he thought
because our nerves
stretch at high speed
and ague follows
sure as thunder
follows lightening. He predicted
the abomination that's Versailles
with its planate boulevards
and arrogant, string-straight ways. No wonder
the queen and her king grew silly
and lost track

of the hungry, little people
underfoot. They were
traveling too fast
too often walking
in straight lines, never needing
to lower their parasols
and look down.

We should have listened
to Master Wren. City block
after city block
of straight lines
and the only time
I need to look down
is when side-stepping
the broken brown bottles
and stinking bodies
sleeping.

FOUR MEN, THREE DOGS, WALKING

> *"A good man is hard to find," Red Sammy*
> *said. "Everything is getting terrible."*
> Flannery O'Connor
> *A Good Man is Hard To Find*

Here
they come, one from
that seafoam mansion
up the way, a second
from the redwood bungalow
with the flowering cherry tress
along its drive, and this one here
come regular as dust
from some far off side street, all
converging on the greenbelt a tick before dawn
to watch their dogs
do their business, the animals
jerked rudely from their dog dreams
and marched yawning
to this frost-covered common, a manicured
patch of grass under siege.

The men
look good, seem fit, and smell good
too, just-shaved
and splashed
with perfumed alcohol, ready
in their sparkling white shirts
and suit jackets
for commerce. The dogs too
are coiffured, smallish, lead housebound lives, each
ridiculous I imagine
with a pheasant in its mouth.

The dog-man teams
take up their accustomed posts

on the greenbelt, all
without bark or greeting, not so much
as a nod or wag between them. This
is business, and after
that circling, sniffing dance
which is the private grace of dogs, the business
is done, even the turds
shockingly neat, manageable, scooped
up, tucked away
in plastic grocery bags.

These are
from all visual cues
decent men, but their muteness
and the precious way
they steer their dogs, are troubling
the way a ringing telephone
in the deep of night
is troubling. These
are the nestle-cocks
of their gender, and though I'm sane enough
to know
the temerity of inviting war, these men need
hatchets in their hands, or failing that
The Misfit bearing down on them
in their rearview mirrors.

In an hour
the sun will be up high enough
to defrost the grass, erase
the paw and shoe prints, and all evidence
that they were ever here
will be gone, which
in the case of these three
and their dogs
is probably best.

HIS HOLINESS, WALKING

Here he comes, descending
from the plane, very round
and slow, and in his infirmity
and white robes, looking and moving
like a glacier
that has seen too much in its years
of inching along
through humanity, through
the seas of frenzied, malnourished
brown, black (but oddly few yellow)
bodies, in his bubble-topped car, the seas
waving at him
as he waved back in that
peculiar, metronomic nodding of the arm
reserved by all cultures of the world
just for him.

But in this scene
he's walking, flanked
by the giant red wings
of two cardinals buoying him up
at the elbows, His Holiness
in that right-leaning, hunchbacked pinch
that is the clearest indication
that the bones
are coming undone
and it won't be long
until he, too, is a footnote
to suffering.

What stands out
is the plain wooden cane
planted firmly ahead
of each glacial footfall, His Holiness

looking for everything
like lovesick Quasimodo
entering
Esmeralda's tomb.

MAN, WALKING

Out here, with nothing
for six miles in either direction
save spindly mangroves
and swirling road dust, is a man
walking. He's walking
against the grain of cars
and smoking trucks with his eyes
forward, a message
that he has no intention
of wooing a ride. There's something
of the egret about him, a gangly man
and each stride long, a flicker
of pause
at the end of each footfall. He's
traveling light, just
a wrinkled paper sack
under an arm.

And that
is all I know
about him, except to say
that I envy him his walk alone
on this desolate road, the elegance
of his task: six miles (at least)
on foot, his only company
the kinesthesia of walking, the chyme
in his gut, and the machinery
of his mind
ticking through the mundane
and profane, 'til all that's left
is that terrible terrible aloneness
that leads
to saving acts
of the imagination:

Her nakedness is sprinkled
with honeysuckle blossoms.
Suddenly her nipples sprout lips
that sing, "there was nothing
before you."

The red sky is full of white birds
shitting sapphires into my mouth.

My children will never die.
I see them standing on a bluff
watching the sun explode. They are
flash-forged into sapphires
plucked from the air
by white birds.

Hell, this could be Homer
walking home, the dazzling
red and green eyes
of four chimeras in his sack, gifts
for his wife and children.

HIS PEDAL GO CLICK, CLICK, CLICK

1. The Physician

I have
a bad prostate: enlarged, mushy, scarred. When I'm
thick with anxiousness, caffeine, alcohol, rage, guilt or
some gymnastic abuse of sex, the doughnut-shaped gland
squeezes off the urethra, cinches like a lariat, a noose
around the exit for both urine and semen, threatens
to back me up like a sewer, poison
my kidneys, liver, kill me
with the waste of my life.

So again I go to the clinic, admit all these sins
to the woman at the computer. She enters me, enters
this all.

The old nurse tears off the blood-smeared tissue
covering the examining table, spreads out
a fresh palette. She has my chart in her hand
but still asks the question:

    So, what can we help you with today?

I tell this mother confessor everything:

    It hurts to urinate. It hurts
    to ejaculate. The cramping
    is vicious.

She notes this on the chart
and in her heart, which I know
because I watch the lines of her face
shift as she leaves
without looking
at me.

I have on
my best underwear.

I wait a long time
in the cold room
on the cold table, playing out
in my head
what I know is coming, the bending
over into a dog, the indignity, the pain.

What sails in through the door
booming, laughing
perhaps at a colleague's joke
or perhaps at my underwear
is a squat, thick-chested black man
in a lab coat stained
with his day's work, a stethoscope
'round his neck like a feather boa.

Although he has the chart in his hand
he asks me the question in a milky voice:

    So, what seems to be the problem?

I tell him everything. Although it's rehearsed, is haunted
by the ghosts of a hundred tellings, I strain to be comforted
when he tells me
that eighty percent of men
suffer this.

As he snaps on the latex glove, he reminds me
of what I already know: *This will hurt.*   I bend
at the waist, lower my best underwear
to my knees, rest my elbows on the table, take the last breath
I'll take for two minutes. He slides
an index finger into my rectum, lubed with jelly
to ease him in, to sweeten me.   He prods

and probes. The pain is awful. At its most awful
this is when I ask him in a squeaky voice

Tell me. Have you ever wanted to do this
to every white man in the world?

The image in my head
is of his lifting me up to the full
extension of his arm, like Atlas, spinning me
on the tip of his finger like a ball
on the wet nose of a seal.

He stops his prodding, but leaves
his finger there, resting. There are
exactly two breaths
between my question
and his response.

Yes

he says, his voice lowered
and thickened

Some days I do. And some days
all white women and children, too.

He exits me gently, snaps off
the latex glove streaked
with what my body rejects.

It's infected

he says, back to business. Enlarged
and mushy as I knew it was.

2. The Cyclist

I still have
a good back, good legs. I can lift
heavy things and could shovel
dirt or manure all day
if there was need anymore
for my back. After forty years
of lifting, bending and unbending
under a load, all that I put my muscles to now
is powering a bicycle, fifteen hundred dollars
of slick steel, power it over mountains
in a canary shirt, shiny black pants
with a purple stripe down the thigh, another
purple streak on the helmet. I am

  Peacock Toucan Cockatoo
   Macaw Bowerbird

sculpting the vanity that firm legs
will set some woman to dancing on my body.

Often I ride at dawn, through the fog, past
acres of mist-mantled strawberry fields, orchards
of yellow apples. Most mornings, when I
reach the road-fall where the fog
is coldest, thickest, I hear a

  click click click

pinging in the fog, growing
in seriousness as it comes on. What slides
out of the fog
is a man on a bicycle, like me
and not like me, his bicycle
a relic of green, peeling paint, stuffing
leaking from the seat, its power
looking blankly ahead, churning and clicking

in iambic pentameter, the brim of his hat
curled up by the wind, a crumpled lunch sack
in one hand, a grimy water jug
dangling from the handlebars, drumming
against the bicycle frame, and a twisted crank, a bent pedal
clicking against the chainstay
with every revolution.

But what is startling about him
is a pink bandana, coiled
and tied tightly 'bout his neck.

All this I see in

    one thousand and one
    one thousand and two
    one thousand and three

seconds. By the fourth
he is gone, has entered
the fog in my wake.

To and from here and there in my truck
I look for him among the men and women
bending and unbending like oil wells nodding
in the fields and orchards
cradling baskets
and canvas bags and boxes, loaded
and heavy.   Some days
I think I see a flash of pink, a man
with a pink bandana 'round his neck. But
there are so many bodies roiling in the fields like snakes
that I am never certain.

I fed myself with my back, bending
and unbending under load, for twenty-five years. Back then
I rode a blue bicycle

with peeling paint and tires
slick and fat as fed pythons. So
do I know
or can I say I know
the man with the pink bandana
riding his bicycle each morning
through the fog?   No, because his pedal go

    click   *click*   *click*

while my pedal go *hummmmmmm.*

SAVING ACTS OF THE IMAGINATION
August 12, 1998

Dear Lamb Chop
is dead, which means
the diminutive, red-haired genius
which was
the innards of the lamb
is dead, too. This might not
mean much to you, but
to the autistic farm boy
from Indiana, this death
in the newspaper
puts me lower
than a skunk, saddens me
more than your death
ever will. 'Cause
when the button-eyed sock talked
I listened, and heard in its voice
the sanction
to be strange, a salving voice
which calmed the terrors
and choked off
the night sweats. The redhead
said it was all right to
go outside of yourself and talk
to your hand, pretend
that it was a sweet lamb
who was awkward as crutches
but who always meant well
and couldn't understand
the cruelty of people.

Which led
to Mary, the bald
and naked girl-dwarf that lived
under my bed and shared my head

and all those
terrible hours under trees
or under the new hay
in the barn, rode
on my shoulder
as I fought through
the forest of cornstalks
or the thicket of scrub
covering the fallow field.

We talked. She
was the only one
who could fathom
the thick stutter, didn't yell
or hit you
upside the head.

Truth be told
she rode my shoulder
until sex
was more interesting
and she became fat
and too heavy
to carry.

There's much more
to tell, but it goes with me
to the crematorium, 'cause
in retrospect
it unnerves me
that she was real as pain
and necessary
as blood.

Isolation and rage
are brutal
to young neurons

and surviving sometimes requires
a saving act
of the imagination. The redhead
knew this, told a quiet boy
and he
is passing the word on to you.

THE WEIGHT OF A CHIID

Way out here
at the hot peak of summer, a day
so hot even the bugs
lay low, way out here
a solid seven miles
from town
on a road used only
by the cranky, by white trash, by people
who hate people, by me, used only
by the occasional growling truck
loaded to the axle with
too-ripe tomatoes, way out here
here's this tall, gaunt woman, hatless, her hair
flying wild
around her face, her dark, heavy clothes
wet with sweat, striding
with insane energy, her purpose kicking up
a rooster tail of dust behind her
as she streaks along
way out here
carrying a pale child, a
skinny boy asleep
or sick
or dead, hanging limp
from the woman's furious hug, her interlocked arms
white, bloodless
with the boy dangling
shoeless to her knees, his bare feet
jerking to and fro as she marches
way out here
to somewhere certain
and I lighten in the heavy heat of noon
knowing
that the weight of this child
is not mine, is not my business
way out here.

KINESTHESIA

Back then, before
living had become mostly pain
and dis-ease, before my spine
went crooked and
my left eye died, back when everything

muscles, bones and brain

worked together so beautifully, back
before such nostalgias were maudlin, there
were moments, odd seconds
when the simple act of moving
was a joyful thing. Sometimes
as a boy on my back in the grass I
would simply stretch my arms up
toward the treetops and listen
to my brain speak eloquently
to my shoulders, elbows, wrists.

Cottonweed fluff lived
in my joints those days, and a brightness
sung in every firing of a nerve. On some days then
throwing a stone or a stick
was a holy thing
my body worshiped. My arm
was a deft whip snapping. My eyes
saw through to forever.

And running. There was that day
that moment
running at full bore
past old Yoder's auto wrecking yard
when everything turned
to slow motion, when
I saw old Yoder's black dog slowly wink

and saw the telephone pole inch by frame
by frame. In that moment
I felt no pain, felt
nothing at all, not even
the road beneath my feet. It was the moment
I suspect
that death whispered to me
for the first time, both a warning
and a celebration.

THE SONG OF BRICKS FALLING

I in my full voice was made
by lightning
shattering the pine tree
and the chickencoop, by bolts
so charged with living
that one blistering flash and its roar
blew a foot and three fingers
from the body of Elsa Bontrager
as she hung her husband's bleached shorts
on the line,

My vocal cords tuned early on
by a pail of warm water and a rag, me
on my hands and knees
next to my father, sponging up the birdshot
and my uncle's exploded head
from the outhouse floor,

The first tones pinched
by playing at manhood, accepting
fifty dollars to help Stevie Carney
unload eleven bodies
from a flatbed truck
and lay them side by side on the dance floor
at the Elk's club, eleven bodies wrapped
in green cloth, bodies torn loose
from their moorings on the planet
by a tornado, a black wind that
plucked them up and crushed them
against the laughing ground,

Eleven: this one with brown stuff
seeping through the green cloth
at the head end, that one
an Amishman's boot tearing through

the cloth as we strained to lift. We managed
eleven bodies
'til the clacking, displaced bones and the smell
sent Stevie bolting into the alleyway
to wretch,

The first clear note formed
by the sight of fifteen hundred suffocated chickens
littering the dooryard, their feathers ruffled
by the afterwinds, their lungs stolen
by the vacuum of a funnel of air and dust
spinning
at three hundred miles per hour,

Formed by the plucking of fifteen hundred hens
in the moonlight, their feathers softened
in washtubs squatting over coal fires, the smell
of the wet feathers forever on my hands,

The first song startled out of my throat
by the act of gripping the crowbar
and prying
with all the stuffing I could muster
against my mother's yelping, to free
her pulpy breast
from the sprung wringers
of the washing machine,

Songs coaxed out of me
by the little murders, my father
cracking a two-by-two
across my forearm, the force
sending a splinter of bone
singing through my shirtsleeve,

By my urine freezing in a glass jar
by my bed, and fevers that played over me
like idiot children banging at pianos,

By the snow
in nineteen fifty-seven, drifting, sealing us into the house
for six days,

And by the ice storm in sixty one
that cast everything
in shining slick crystal, sent Samuel Yoder
shooting through the windshield
of his new Plymouth Coupe, the sun—when it
showed itself—melting the ice
but not the glass,

By reading the libretto
of Enos Miller's beard
and all his face from ear to ear
torn off and tangled in the blade
of the bandsaw, the sight of Enos
careening around the barn, clutching
the exposed, oddly-jutting jawbone, by his
hideous teeth and gums, by my second knowing
that the bones of the living
are yellow, not white,

By the hymn of a calf, my slim arm
stretched down the birth canal
of the heifer, my hair soaked by the work
of hacksawing, the wet, slippery quartering
of the calf dead two days there
and stinking,

By the one great bass note
of my son, an eleven pound bawling lump
schlumping out from his mother,

And schooled
by my father's thundering insistence
that I stiffen my back, place

the blue muzzle of the rifle into the ear
of the milk cow, punish it for the bad luck
of breaking a leg
in the slats of a cattle crossing, the bang
muffled to a gush as the penny-sized bit
of elemental lead
sloshed its way through the cow's fat head
and out its cheek.

So it is
that when the earth quakes, plays dreidels
with the church steeples
and the chimneys, I wish
with the grandest, saddest song I know
that the bricks would all fall, all fall down, while I
whirl like a dervish on the lawn, breathing deeply
of the swirling dust, stomping my feet
and shocking to death all the neighborhood
and all the dissonance
therein
and within.

IF NOT FOR BIRDS

One hundred species of songbird
I'm told
now near to disappearing. Better
to kill the cats and the dogs
and the little boys with BB guns
for I have determined
that living without birds
wouldn't be living.

From their perch
on the telephone wires
the red-winged blackbirds
send up a great racket, a bit like
a knot of burbling, frothing
children in the park, annoying in their energy
while also
cheering you on. Whether in chorus
or from a single note
streaking through the redwoods, it is
the word of bird that I listen for
as I walk. Who else
to teach me to whistle again
as I grow old
and blind?

THE FLOWER WITH THE PRICKLY STEM

On our walk
my learned friend, the scholar
points a bony finger
at each bright blossom
and kills each with its name:

Heliotrope.
Pectocarya.
Fiddleneck.
Trillium.
Owl's Clover.
Sage.

His naming boils
each beautiful flower down
to a referent
which has no eyes. From
this naming moment on
I no longer see
the flower with the prickly stem or
the red bloom that catches bugs
in its sticky cup
or the wispy yellow blossom
that dances like Martha Graham
when the wind's up. I no longer bend down
and see
the pink dust which gathers
on the little hairs that poke up
where the lavender, sword-shaped petals
meet the flower's heart. From then on I walk
quickly through my garden, call up the file

FLOWERS

click off the names like
a playing card
clicking over the spokes
of a bicycle wheel.

In the old cemetery
there is a small gravestone
which says only

    Pieteranella Hoogerhyde

and I wonder, did they ever note
her splendid white hands, the grace
in her gait, the way she always smiled
at children? When my friends say

    Joseph

or think

    Joseph

what little magnificence
do they miss, what small danger
do they rend away? Am I more beautiful
to strangers
passing on the street?

GOODBYE, CATHY CAMPBELL

In my fiftieth year
she disappears. Try
as I might
I can no longer
conjure her up at will
in my naps, materialize
her lithe body and clay smell
in my mind's bed
over coffee and croissant.

Odd. For years
I wanted her expunged, wished
her ill, say a skin condition
or children
with horribly bad teeth, payment
for the pain and
fitful sleep. But
she still came calling
while I shaved or
stood in line at the bank. Hands
I wanted so much on me, a mouth
and a filed-smooth voice
that could turn me
willingly to salt. She taught me
the possibilities of the body
and flushed the Pope and Jesus
from my skin. Aloud
we read Nin and Miller
while *Kind Of Blue*
set things up
for our bodies.

But the husband. What to do
with the husband? He threw
great pots

and never hit her. He went to Nam
while I studied Kierkegaard
and Williams. He had qualities
the way that common moths
have color
and Blue Gill fish are great
when breaded and fried. But
he didn't *do* it for her
the way I did, which for years
was all that trumpeted me
in the world.

She made
the good decision, though I'm told
she went her way away finally
to the mountains
with a big bricklayer
to have his kids.

Now
her face is a smudge
and I have no photographs, no
refresh button to click. What comes up
fuzzily a last time on the monitor
is her reddening white bottom, rising
and falling, the bog smell, her
whimpering, the impossibly long, fine fingers
gripping the blue footboard. And I cannot
feel a thing.

COMMON GROUND

The courageous thing to do
would be to slip this
under the salt shaker
with your tip.

But I can't, stymied by a feeling
that we share a common ground richer
than the unmade beds and the dishes
in our sinks, a feeling
that you're a sister
they never told me about, that you were
kidnapped from the farm and driven
3,000 miles to this drab diner
perched on the cusp of Bluett Pass, that someone
stove in your spirit, too, drained
all pleasure from your body, drove you
like a pile-driver setting posts
into a stoop and shuffling step.

For two years I have watched your
every pirouette and curtsy, watched
like a scientist
how your elbow reached for heaven
as you poured coffee, recorded
every milk-toned, cabbaged, gutless
greeting you ever made
to the cook or the customers. And
there was the dream
where you served me
breakfast in bed: you were naked, white
as a swan you were
with great swatches of nothing
dark holes
at every point on your body
where you'd ever been less than loved.

One morning
I swear
I could see the ghosts of fingers, welts
running across your neck, the tell-tale signs
of our addiction to constant reenactments
of the little brutalities, our habitual couplings
with surrogate spirit crushers, hench-parents.

It's your face that betrayed you, the doe eyes
that looked anywhere
but at the faces of others
and those hands
that were never sure of where they belonged.

Once, I tried to say good morning
but couldn't, tried once
to talk to you
about the treacherous black ice
on the pass, rehearsed once
a compliment
on your new haircut. But each time
my voice tangled in the muck, bogged down.

So, in silence I loved you, in pieces: first
your hands, slender and you-don't-know
how lovely, always
looking to hide. Then
your arms, the shoulders carried so low
that they nearly ceased being shoulders. Then
finally
your neck, your cheeks, graced I'm certain
too seldom by kisses.

On my last day
over the pass, I take your eyes
out of your head, cup them

gently in my hands, then salt them
and eat them.

Forgive me. A small audience of strangers
will read of my affection for you. All I can do
is eat your eyes
and tip you generously, frozen
and buried as I am
in the same ground.

FIVE WITH K . H .

1. **Alice Adams**

With Fred MacMurray
*(1935)   ***1/2*

I might be wrong
here
but I can't imagine that sex
with this woman
could ever [have been]
good
good the way say
sex with myself is good, can't imagine
this skinny, whiny, cloying girl
ever pleasantly sweaty astride me, riding
my big bull cock, hot. If I push the image, maybe
but feel her insides dry as ashes, fighting
my wetness
the way oil fights water.

Fred knew this, too. You can see it
in the trembling blankness of his speech
at the dinner table, see in his flat eyes
over hot soup on a hot day
the wish only for possession
of the beautiful, repulsed
by the scheming energy
of her silly body.

Run, Fred, run
back to the socialite with bad teeth
but with a humid sex
big as a cow's
and a grip
strong as Delilah's.

2. Stage Door

With Adolphe Menjou
*(1937)   **1/2*

I'm ugly
so the only way I can touch her, smell
her neck and what lives
in that dark place, is to shimmy at three a.m.
up the drain pipe, pry open
the window, hoist my trembling body through the window
and into the hallway. Four rooms, each
holding ruddy warm flesh rich
as any mink, the breasts not moving
what with the shallow breaths of the deep-sleeping.

Four doors. Lucy
behind one. K. H.
behind another. Ann
and Eve, roomies. My body tells me Lucy, red-haired
even in black and white, sturdy and open
as a passion flower. With Ann and Eve, dancing
of course
and straight vodka
and three-part renderings
of big band songs.

But like an ant to sugar it is K. H.'s door
I push open, slip into the room like
carbon monoxide creeping.

It is not
what you think. I'm no Adolphe, come
for the coming. I'm here to touch what
lives under her swooshing
hair, what camps like Napoleon's armies
inside her skull. I'm here
to wonder at the lightning I'm certain crackles

through her brain as she sleeps, touch
the searing air
which roils off her head in great waves
even in dream, the ephemeral stuff
which makes the risk of bad sex
and cold acting and lousy dancing worth
the terrible longing.

3. Pat and Mike

With Spencer Tracy
(1952)   ***

My heart is berserk, insane
as I read the note, stained
with her sweat (it was hot
today, at Augusta). We've
agreed to meet this suffocating
hot night, on the green
at Number Eight.

Even
in the moonless night, I can see her
white shorts and white tank top
coming up the fairway, coming ghostlike
to me, to my waiting lips. She walks straight
to me, certain that my body
is all she'll ever want
or need. Panting, she spills
into my arms. I can feel the wet hotness
of her body and the Georgia night
wash over me as we fall
to the grass. She grabs my big bull cock
with both hands, sucks me into her, thrusts
screaming, awakening the birds.

Tracy
she knows now

is soft and weak
and not the food
her body
all these years
has been starving for.

4. The Lion in Winter

With Peter O'Toole
(1968)   ****

This is K. H. the technician, all
wheels and pulleys
and gears, the beautiful body

    (yes, still liquid and enticing
    as cool water
    even as her face falls and the hands
    tremble with disease)

the beautiful body
still there under the folds
of silk and sequins
but now only
a costumed burn to torture
stupid men. Hopkins
as the bisexual son, Richard, still
wants her, and she knows
he wants her, so pricks him
with edgy words and a look
which runs the full five feet
from his eye
to his member. Poor Henry
knows her power, too, so locks her tired womb
in the tower.

I watch all this
from behind the great tapestry

of Henry the First sacking
some poor French village. I plan
to rescue her, take her
on my big black horse
to my cottage
where we'll peel back
her sequined satin
and strip off my smelly sack-cloth shirt
and make good England
the heir
it deserves.

5. Mrs. Quigley

With Nick Nolte
*(1983)   *1/2*

Now the truth
comes out. It's the assassin in K. H.
I love, her sterile black heart, the cold hands
that poison the old, ill, sad and scarred. In the way
that the condemned
come to feel longing
for their executioners, I want
her black body, the one
so close to death. Nick
never knew why
he followed her, but
I do. Can there ever be sex
as good as this ? all pain
escaping like air from a tire
as she rides me and
twists her panties ever more tightly
around my neck, all the time
sneering down at me, her red face
clearly now
the spitting image
of my mother's.

KILLING THE WARRIOR

Standing naked
before the mirror
I find the warrior
even in my old body, see myself
running this leanness full tilt
across the white-hot savanna, spear
in hand, gaining
on some lame, sorry Springbok
or a slower man
I've been taught to hate. If I
twist my torso just so
the muscles and the tendons
rustle, stir from their hiding places
within the flesh, define themselves again
even in my old body.

Though
I've never killed a man
I know that I could
and maybe even feel sick pleasure
as I held the bastard's trophy heart
above my head and howled, licked
his blood from my hands.

And don't be fooled
by my clean, smooth hands. I am
a man of violence, a warrior hemmed in
by guilt and law, suffocated by all this civility
barking at me like an idiot dog. I
have been taught violence
the way a tongue-talented child
is taught words, daily
through the mayhemish small acts
of those henchpeople
who shared my name.

But without a hunt
or sanctioned war, I folded
the brutality within, carved up
my insides, trashed
the chambers of my heart, poisoned
my own blood. I smelled of rot
and the taste of bile
was in my speech.

Then
across the room she came, soft
as an anemone, but strong inside too
like an anemone, took hold of me
and patient as rust and sweet-breathed whispered
six thousand times with her moth-must hands
you will stop this; you're too old
for war; it doesn't suit you and
if you don't stop, your goodness
will be eaten up, you will be empty
and you will echo inside
like a schoolyard
on Sunday. Over and over
until I did, I put down
the spear one day, curled up
within the shade
of a big oak, closed my eyes
and slept, mewing in my sleep
like a cat
circling a bowl of fish heads.

For ten thousand years
the shes have been whispering such
to us, though no archeologist yet
has written down
the truth of the matter, because

there is no evidence like a bone
to pull from the dirt
and wave around in the air
like a scalped ticket to paradise.

~ 53 ~

AT THIS TIME

of the bright, workday mid-morning when
the streets and the beach are quiet, after
the cars have long since cut their sick paths
to work, the kids are dying somewhere
in a big brick building and The Sears Man
has come with the new fridge and gone, after
all this, out come the broken and twisted
to air themselves, without work
as they are, unable to obey the clock
or abide the foreman, their brains
terribly mis-chemicaled (or some
in motorized chairs, their legs
cut out from under them
by shrapnel, disease, chain saws, or
fate of birth).

Because they brave
the brightest light of day
they all have
strawberry skin
or wear their rage as a red rash
on their cheeks
and the backs of their hands. They are all
scarecrow skinny and walk Chaplin fast
and erect, shake
and sway like blown-around saplings
as they loiter at the corners of all
the Main and Pine streets
in the world, talking to their shoes, shades, or
sadly, God.

I watch them
from a crack in the blue-flowering hedge, myself
with no place to go
and only a weighed dry ounce

of flesh to shed
before I take up my post
on some corner or other
and sway heel to toe with finally
someone to talk to.

HARUSPEX

I've come through the hooting cold wind
and cutting sleet
to buy a chicken
from the sour-jawed, one-eyed butcher
who never speaks but to tell you
he hasn't cheated you, his scales
are true.

Always
when you turn to leave
this high priest of flanks and chops
says *Hey!*
and you turn back to him, a chill
creeping across your skin, to see
his fat hands held high
and spread, his amber gleaming glass eye
trained on you
like a flashlight. *Hey!* He smiles. *A butcher 35 years*
and I still got
all my fingers.

Today, as the bell makes its final
flat-ringing slap against the door, I find myself
alone in the shop. He is not at his stool
behind the great bleached block. Today
I'm greeted only by
the naked headless fowl, the mangy
milk-eyed trout and the stacks
of browning fat-edged steaks.

Just as I raise my hand
to thwap the counter bell I hear
voices murmuring, sad-lilted and murky, slipping
to me through a six-inch cracking
of a door I've never noticed before.

Always the voyeur, I move
close to the crack, peep into
the cold, meat-rank dimness of a room
clotted with waxy brown boxes and
stinking scrap barrels and graying
mottled slabs of once-cows hanging
on hooks, all lit nastily
by one bleak bulb.

Under the weak light
stand the one-eyed butcher
and a dashing state trooper, both
staring up quite awed
at a mangled brown something
that used to be an elk, hanging
by its front hooves
on a ceiling hook.

What's left of its crushed head
lolls toward me, the eyes and muzzle
obliterated by a trauma. A piece of tongue
squirts from the frozen wound. Its hide is caked
with mud and dripping ice. A reddish puddle
forms on the floor near where the rear hooves
dangle. Slivers of glass, embedded
in the torn, crushed head
shine, catch the light
from the dull bulb.

The damn dumb animal

the trooper mutters.

The sixth road kill in three days

he says to his boots.

*Trucker said it came on to him
like it was magnetized. Her head
exploded when it hit. Jesus
but they're dumb animals*

he says to his hands.

The meat's probably ruint

the butcher says, then pulls
a dressing knife from his apron and
with one stroke
tears her tan belly
north to south. As the knife works down
out slip the gleaming snakes
of her insides, glopping into coils
of brilliant green and purple and yellow
at their feet.

The trooper lights a cigarette and I
feel nothing. But the butcher, he crouches and stares
at the steaming coils with his good eye, studies them
a long time.

Before I call out to you, ring
the bell and claim my frying hen, tell me
butcher, haruspex, what do you read
in the tangle, the cast
of her entrails? Are we
in as much trouble
as I think we are?

SNAKE, BAT, SPIDER, SHARK, BOY

I've killed
a Stellar's Jay, shot it just now
clean and dead through the head
with my son's pellet gun
as the black and blue beast squawked
from its perch on
the bird feeder, crumbs of millet
flying from his beak
as he fell. I did this
on the sly, stalking him day after day
when my wife was away
and my son at school, calculated, pre-
meditated, reasoning that his racket
outside my window at precisely sixteen
minutes after dawn was a danger
to my sleep, to my health.

Let's be honest
here. Each year I kill
some blooded thing, always
as well-reasoned
as the tie I choose
to go
with my pink shirt.

Mark this with the image
of me age nine, standing astride
a nest of blue racer snakes
screaming

    sonsabitches
    sonsabitches
    sonsabitches

as I hacked each blue-streaked wriggling baby
in two with my Barlow. Or
the cool-browed way at eleven
I slaughtered for market
that week's quota
of frying hens, feeling efficient
as I whistling strung the last flailing headless whiteness
from the clothesline, my mongrel black dog
licking the blood from my boots
as I worked.

This
is not a nostalgia, but a deep
and terrifying puzzlement which shakes me
to my toes. Perhaps
it's something cellular, or printed in India Ink
on the brain, stamped
like the mark of Satan
on my life.

Too many times in poems, men
as boys
kill things and reflect and whimper and gnash teeth
and shrug. I say
continue, always, to be afraid. Keep
the door bolted
while you teach peace
to your children. Carry
a rock in your pocket
as you walk home
in the dark.

SEVEN

In this class
there are seven, not dwarfs
but large boys, their bodies
fully formed, but as men
still in rehearsal. They sit each
dangerously quiet, heavy-lidded as frogs, sprawled
like throw rugs in their chairs, usually
without books or paper or pens. I do not know
what they come for
but come they do when the sun and moon
are right in aspect, steam
hissing from their bored bodies
as they slide slickly into their chairs.

Misery loving company, I
huddle them together to discuss
the reading, which no one
has done, and the assignment, which
not one has begun. Loving as Abraham
I join them, pull up a chair
and put on the air
of a man
looking back at boyhood. We talk in mumbles
of automobiles, gaming and girls. Each
is frightening in his simplicities, the
terrifying clarity
with which they draw their lines, the
awful energy
barely under harness, wasted
in this room
of books and chalk.

Does anyone out there
need a bridge built
or a city torn down

in a day? I have
your crew. All you'd need
are seven hammers, seven
saws, a pencil, seven
framing squares, a bag
of six-penny nails and
seven sack lunches. Maybe too
in thanks
a bag of hard candy, a pony keg
and a boom box playing anything loud
as the sun settles down.

FUH Q

Some little linguist
with wiry hair just newly springing
from the root of his penis, a felon
in rehearsal, has done this violence
to the sign post, to my eyes, to
the ether. I'm guessing that
at home
the parents sit on him
but incompletely, like on
a bulging, too-full suitcase, a pant cuff
and a shirt sleeve
leaking out as the latch goes *click*.

Maybe not blows, but
there have been bruising words
doled out to our artist over time
less carefully than ice cream
or the rare round warm words
that we crave at bedtime
as the covers are tucked in.

Eventually
the rage squirts up, first
as some simple torture
of the cat, later
as the laceration
of self hate.

This one is smart, so makes
as his first public yowl
these four symbols artfully
arranged, rendered
in beautiful silver
and blue, a petty first trickle
before the flood.

SUNNING WITH MY WIFE

She says she can feel
their eyes, the three boys
with the boom box, watching
like seagulls at a picnic, her body
broiling next to me
in the sun, their imaginations
waiting
for some nipple revelation, some
miracle catastrophic strap failure
as she lolls. With her
darkening skin and
canary-yellow suit she is
no doubt
a sight for boys' eyes, out
of their league and untouchable
what with the wrinkled guy
keeping watch
and all these people, these
witnesses all around
cooking on the sand.

For a minute
I try to see
what they see, recapture
the stirring I know
that comes and goes
like the tide
in the swimming trunks
of boys.

And I can. If
they only knew
how sweet her skin
really was, will be
later after her shower

has cooled it, could taste
these blisters of sweat
puddling her lip
and the small
of her back, she would
break their hearts
as crisply
as she has mine.

This instant
I deeply love
these boys, because
if I do not love them
all of this
is more despair
than I care to suffer.

PEEK-A-BOO

I hide my face in my hands
wait a heartbeat
then spring open my fingers, pop out
like Jack from his box, play the ancient game
of here-and-gone-and-here-and-gone
with my granddaughter.

She will outlast me, could
play this game for hours. The game
is new to her, but I
am weary of it, having already learned
the terrible business
embedded in the sport, am turned
cloudy and sullen as Lent
by its serious turn.

Presence
and absence
are big things, big
as houses, bigger than
hot and cold or
tall and short, big
as *happy and sad* and maybe
even bigger than *living and dead*
'cause you can hold the dead
in your arms
at least for a while, note
the absence of breath.

The brain
is clever in its needs.

This talk show doctor
says here-and-gone
is one of the first ideas

a child comes to maybe
in the abstract. How else
to endure

   mummy was here
   and now she's gone

to the market, to work, to
a movie? How else to prepare
for the awful peek-a-boo
of cemeteries and crematoriums
than by way of
this child's game? To be game
is to be doughty and plucky, no?

Today
I am playing teacher. My granddaughter
is learning
to be heroic.

IN THE MANNER OF LIONS

There are six
or seven children swarming
on the riverbank, radiating out
then returning, yo-yoing
out-and-back in a frenzy
from the short, muscled man
their maypole. They are
miniatures of him, strong
and alive as milk-mouthed kittens.

Here on the bank of the turgid river
their aliveness horrifies him, his face gnarled
into alarm, his voice barking
at this one and that. One, wide-eyed, dips
a hand into the broil, another
climbs too high up the rock.

Although his powerful body, still
and stout, is a post we could all tether to, his head
pivots in the manner of lions, taking in
all the dangers of the plain, and
like those lions, manes flaring, their mouths
flaming with the blood of their own, the urge
is to eat the slow one, the frail one, to call back
a few of the single-minded seedings.

In the truck, under
the potholed seat, there is a rifle
wrapped in an oiled rag. The scrub
is dense along the riverbank.

If only there had never been
an Abraham, or a carpenter
from the House of David.

AT THE FALLS

The last
quarter mile of the trail
is a sad reminder that I
am older than her, a great step closer
to an obituary. My chest
is on fire, my legs
shake from the work. I'm drawn along
in my crab-like scuttling
by the carrots of her white legs
and my ardor, drunk I am
on the sticky fumes left in the air
by her laboring body.

On the farm we had
an old rooster, scruffy
and moth-eaten, more crow and strut
than stud. But persistent as ivy, managing
each day to rouse himself
and work the henyard, bobbing and weaving
through the clucking and the cackling, hoping
desperately
for a raucous tumble in the dust, something
to verify his roosterness.

So after her I huff and claw
up the switchbacks, catching just a flash
of her body before she cuts up the next draw
and disappears, always
just out of sight and achingly
out of touch. What pulls me on
is the promise she's made
and the ever-growing thunder
of the falls.

As I stagger the last yards
I see her
thrust like a masthead
into the spray, the mist
matting her hair and gathering
like frost on her face.   True
as always to her word, she turns and
in one slow elegant motion
peels off her shirt, throws
her arms wide, shows to me, god, the trees and the stones
her perfect breasts, the ones I've been seeing
and kissing in my mind
for four killing miles, the only shame
embedded in her laugh
when I cock back my head
and crow a crow
that drowns out the falls
and all the blind world watching.

WHAT'S NOT SEEN

All the men in this room
are engaged like me
in the craft of imagining
the rest of her breasts, the bodies
of icebergs lurking
below her bust line, under the shroud
of her slick blue rayon shift.

The puffs of flesh
jutting dangerously above the waterline
are lovely, and when she leans
across the table to punch home
a point to her friend
all of us blinkless and breathless strain
to realize our imaginations.

It's usual as dirt
to blame this shameless breast ogling
on our mothers, improper
weaning, as mating matters, as
fire stoking, but that's
selling us short, as if
we were incapable of anything
as grand as envy, or seeing
that great thing that Rubens
or Titian saw, that thing
that drove the best of Rome, Damascus
and the Ming. This
is the most essential
of crafts, as what's not seen
is what's driving
the bus.

IT'S OKAY

Hunched over
this downhill left-to-right breaking
five-foot birdie putt
I can feel your shadow
heavy as guilt on my back. I imagine
that your teeth are clenched
and you're wishing
the way one wishes ill on a neighbor
with a better job
and comelier wife
that I'd miss this putt, want it
to lip just out
to ripen the pain of my failure.

It's okay
to want this. What's left
for warless warriors under the thumb of law
but vacant games that stand in
for the killing in us? Prick this
moth-wing thin veneer
of rules and etiquette
and out bubbles mayhem. It wouldn't
take much
to crush your brain pan
with my three iron, or better yet
something with more loft, say
the eight. Behind the fourteenth green
I saw a wood chipper
to make mulch of you, or maybe
I'll take my time
and dismantle you in the garage, for
science's sake, study the way
the tendons attach to the bones, track
with the knife
the nerve route

from your dick to your brain. Too
I've always thought that your wife
had beautiful skin, and can imagine
those big lips slicked up
with my saliva, working
on me. I entertain
that in your case
no one would notice
your absence, and
after a discreet while
she would come to prefer
the smell of me.

It's
okay. The crimson in us
trumpets always
just under the skin. Because
we share this
I love you
and have every intention
of making this putt.

DESERT BLOOMING

The first thing I see
as I step from the AC
into the choking heat
of the desert at noon
is this woman-child
sitting on a bench, framed by
the filling station window, lapping
at a red popsicle. She's short
of sixteen, weighed down
by the loud belly-evidence
of sex with a man, or
more likely, with a warbling, scabrous
urgent-handed boy more peccary
than peacock, sweaty sex
in some hot place at night
without music or an ohm
of resistance, with his pants
and her panties half on.

Every sausage in the station
is watching her
as she swings her legs
and laps, all already convinced
that they're in love, most
with the sticky red lips, or
with the fresh lusciousness
they know is there
beneath her gauzy peignoir, a few
with the loud belly-evidence, the roaring fire
of some boy's ego
she'll need carry
for life.

Though I wish for her
a palanquin born

by four gentle eunuchs, she's
carried away from us
in her mother's pickup, an old Ford
shot through with rust.

Even if
I followed her, dropped
to my knees, apologized
for all of us, promised her
everything that I had, she is
doomed way out here
in the desert
with nothing to nourish her
but the flickering blue light
of the television I see
through the trailer's window.

MAJIK

I do not have
anywhere in my body
a spiritual bone. The Buddha
was a sad fat man, Yahweh
an asshole
who will be taken to task
if ever I get the chance. But how to explain
the mystery of my wife, this woman
who shares my bed and daily at dusk
the pot of boiled food?

See, I fancy myself a gardener, read
all the books and buy
all the right sprays, potions
and fertilizers. But next to her
I'm the Grim Reaper
for the plant kingdom. It is
a great mystery.

She shares
this love of flowers so
on Saturdays we put on
the stiff hide gloves and pot
all manner of flowering thing. She's kind
so lets me pot
the healthy ones with
the sturdy, knuckle-sized buds, while she
takes on the basket cases, the spindly
polio-ridden brown near-deaths
the nursery gives away. I watch her
like a hawk, do
what she does at each step: air
the soil, fluff it lovingly, scoop out

a plant womb, gently settle in the root ball, add
more soil, tamp gently and water
just so.

Always beautiful beginnings, but
by week's end
it's always the same: her plants
take on a robust rousing green, stand tall
while mine curl
into tight death spirals. For a while
I thought it was her singing, the ditty
she makes up as she works so
I sing, too, but still
mine die. Then
once
I thought I saw her spit
into the hole before she set the plant
so I spit, too, but still
mine go to the trash heap
collecting there like flies to raw meat.

Wiser
after these years of close watching
I know now that it's the poison running up
from my gut and out my fingertips
which does them in. She has
no poison in her
you see
being love in total. The proof
of the majik in her is me
here standing
not bent over as I once was, sturdy now
as a hollyhock and bright as a zinnia
after these years
in her hands.

STIGMATA

She comes in from the rain
with her pants hiked up, bleeding in rills
from the palms and the knees, the little
streams of candy-apple red
thinned and egged on
by the rainwater dripping
from her hair, from her clothes.

Her life stuff
is leaking out
and I'm surprised
at my knee-jerk anger, shocked
to hear me screaming
about her clumsiness, as if falling
were an act of will.

I catch myself, ask
for forgiveness as I fold her
into my arms, make
cerebral pap of it, tell her
that except for rare, seen smears
of menstrual blood, cardinals
landing suddenly in the snow, I
have never seen her bleed.

But really
it goes deeper still, my rage
a selfish thing, narcissism, worry
about my own daily endangerment, moving
as I do as flimsy bones and blood
through the world. I recall for her
my father, hearing
of my sister's death, calmly
loading the rifle, shooting point blank
the caterwauling rooster, then

going to bed early, coward
that he was. Because
I failed her, this woman I love
until I cannot see her
from me, I then tell her
the truth, that
I cannot, finally, protect her, and that
the scars due to form on her knees
are temporary lies, that Christ
was a stud, that he knew the truth
about the holes in his hands
even as he anguished
in the garden. *Trust me*, I say
as she stands white-faced, wet
and shaking before me, *the sorry
son of a bitch
never rose up
from no grave.*

WITH MEN

it is all about always
mortality, how close
or far away you are
from dying, how close
the bullet was when
you dodged it, whether
you could actually feel
the displaced air
lap at your ear
as it passed.

Talking
with men, strangers
all, at a conference lunch, people
I have just met
and will never see again, after dessert
it always comes around
to heart attacks, ruptured discs, MRI's
and urethras caught in the noose
of the prostate. These are
fully-realized men, gray-templed
captains of industry
and the academy, all
in crisp shirts and silk ties, looking
white as porcelain
as they paw
at the raspberry cheesecake, each in turn
reporting in meaty tones
on The State of the Body.

It's in their shorthand, too, that odd nod
men give as they pass other men
on the street, or while zipping up
and flushing the urinal, a curt curtsy
from the neck which says, *See, I'm*

ambulatory. I'm not dead
yet, and if pressed
I could wrestle you
to your knees.

And these are not
stupid men. They can do
the math. They know all about
those troubling granite markers
at the cemetery, the man's name
in place, the space for the wife's
still blank, smooth
and deeply gray. In some cases
the message from the stone
is more disturbing, that the woman
will never share the grave, having
it seems, moved on
to some lucky man still breathing
who will come to wear your shoes
and mistreat
your lawnmower.

What to talk about
with strange men
around the table at lunch
but the prospect
of what there is left
to lose, each body
clinging for all it's worth
to its little bit of space.

THE PRINCIPLE OF VERTICALITY

The very old man
with the crazy white hair
is eating lunch
with his daughter. Now
and then, she smiles too hard
or talks too loud
or reaches over
to cut his pork chop
or butter his bread. These things
he lets her do, resigned
that her daughterly hovering
isn't worth a fuss. But
after the bill's paid
and it's time
to go, he slaps away
her hands, insists
on attaining verticality
on his own.

The whole room
falls silent, watches
the slow uncorking
of his body, and in the silence
we swear we can hear
the clicking of his bones.

For this heroic act of will
it takes a full minute
to overcome the terrible tug
of gravity
but finally he is rod straight
and beautifully perpendicular
to the floor, perfectly
plumb. As an encore

his first step too
is his own.

We all
clap inside. Dessert
is good.

THE PRICE OF POTATOES

In my left hand
is an organically grown
red potato, in my right
one saved from aphids
and burrowing microscopic leggy things
by some petrochemical compound
I cannot pronounce. The commercial spud
is larger than the one grown only
in earth tossed
with steer dung. The small one
costs one twenty-nine per pound, but
I can get the big one and some cousins
for eighty-nine cents per pound.

My day
is as full as a commuter train
with such decisions, while
crawling up my neck like a chigger
is the feeling
that the darkness
is gathering thick all around me
and if I do not act
this instant, if
I don't grab that woman there
grading with a keen eye one by one
a bin of Jonathon apples, if
I don't take her in my arms
and dance with her the merengue
up and down the produce aisle
'til we drop from exhaustion, laughing
and dripping sweat smelling of keytones I
am forever lost to the darkness.

If only
I was not hungry.

STORY

September 1, 1997

The master teacher tells me
that we are slaves
to narrative, that we are chained
always to story, the sequence of events
like links in our chains. We do not dream
in random images
but in story
he says
and in this way
we store our events, catalogue
and process like photographs
the painful and the beautiful
and the strange. This is why
he says
we lap up like dogs water
the lives of others, take on
their chains, go deep into the night
telling and hearing
the little trivialities
of our days, listen, rapt, to Regis Philbin
and Uncle Chuck, his cigarette flicking
in the corner of his mouth
as he talks for hours
about the day
his cows died.

Here's a story:

A privileged, pleasant-faced young English woman
married a prince and thus became a princess. Everybody
noticed, and I mean everybody. She was a bit vacant
and he had frightfully big ears. He wore kilts and she
blue gowns which glittered. They traveled around
doing practically nothing and people with cameras

traveled around with them, clicking and clicking. They
had two male children. The prince and princess spent
a lot of time apart. They had sex with other people.
It was scandalous. They divorced. He took up with an old
girlfriend with a beaked nose. She took up with a
rich Egyptian. One night, after dinner in Paris, the princess
and her Egyptian tried to outrun the guys with cameras
in the Egyptian's black Mercedes Benz. But their drunk
chauffeur plowed them head on into a concrete post. The Egyptian
was fatally lacerated. She was mortally ruptured. There
was a big fuss, which everybody noticed, and I mean everybody.

How
you catalogue this one, in which file
this little story goes, is
a very curious thing.

OF THE PRINCESS, THE AUTOMOBILE, AND BAD ART
September 5, 1997

The same pattern of mind
that fashioned the land mine
and Michael Jackson
made this evil thing, this
monstrosity. Along the way
to inventing a slick way
from here to there, cool industry
bred with a fear of being tied down
by the company of others
and spat out
this grotesque metal boxy thing
on wheels. Now we move
mostly in ones, not even often
in twos and threes, through the snow
to grandma's house
and rain to the movie house
and in a slow sea of such boxes
to our work. It even has lights
to move us at night
to the opera. Some folk
whistle as they roll along and some
sing or pick and fret
from being so much alone.

It was always
a flawed idea, like fascism
and lawn darts, but one day, hey, it
was the only way to get there
and too late
to find another way.

There's no going back
I know
but the wrinkle of *mass times velocity*

equals at least
bad art. Like this photograph on page one
of a wheeled, black, metal thing crushed
by mass, inertia, the immovable, and
too many G's. It's an ugly *objet d'art*
made uglier
by the shredded viscera smeared inside
on the windows and the seats. This box
didn't just kill, it
ruptured regal aortae
and sheared away faces
and exploded heads like casabas
under the feet of elephants.

I don't mourn much the lives
(there are so many more people
waiting) but I do mind
my curiosity in the twisted lines
of this mangled, metal box, in how our brains
re-invented its use, while my dog, squatting
to take a shit, invents nothing
but a grin. I study this, this sculpture
too long
as if this bad art
had something important
to say.

CAMERA GRAVIS

September 6, 1997

Like funerals
cameras
are for the living. So
what are cameras
at funerals but proof
that death is all that's interesting
finally, the camera, the photo, a clevis
between a deep, black unspeakable fear
and the sweet anticipation of supper, a bowl
of soup and a piece of bread.

An old, drunk Irish poet, nearly
the cliché, warned me: never
write about death but obliquely, only
as euphemism. Too slippery he said
to ever roll it up neatly
like a clew
in language.

But photographs
have a chance at least to safely build
a morbid celestory from which
to watch the proceedings, like viewing
an autopsy, frozen. All these
puffy-eyed Brits standing
along the route
of this silly woman's procession
clicking away
between sobs, clicking at catafalque
casket, black drape and flowers
but in the darkest part of dream
wanting to be sure, wanting
to see her torn face, the obscenity
and the awful, gospel truth.

WHEN IT HAPPENS

Though I've been taught
it's a silliness, I do not like
living out of earshot of you. I tremble
too
when you break free
from my sight line. Each day
the car starts up and I sicken
at you
without me
floating down the road in a horrible tin box
suspended from the hard road only
by four rubbered wheels, at the mercy
of the villainous bad tempers of others flying
at dismembering speeds
in their tin boxes.

When you cough
I cringe. When you prick a finger
draw blood
I die more
than a little. When you catch a cold
I know certainly
pneumonia is not far off. I see you
ash-colored
in a small starched bed, dying
in little gasps, spittle gathering
at the corners of your mouth, your
fish-like hand
cold and still in mine.

I envy those men
in the cemetery who share
death dates with their mates, and Heifitz
that foofy-haired Russian violin player
who boasted that in 55 years

he
and his beloved had
never slept apart.

Perhaps
somewhere
there is a physician
with the needles and the sutures and the skill
to whip-stitch us together, preferably
at the belly
or the lips. Maybe
you'll let me take you down
into the dark and terrible basement
where there's carpenter's glue
and a staple gun.

Please, something
anything
to ensure that I'll be there
when the necessary tragedy
happens by.

WHAT GOES IN

My scholar friend
is repulsed by mouths, these gashes
we stuff with meat
and things we grow in dirt. He does not
kiss his wife and
refuses to vomit, which is hard 'cause
the sight or thought of teeth, what
they're for, makes him ill. (Tongues
are fine he says
as they give us talk
which is his life.)

With me
it's not the mouth itself
that is obscene, but it as metaphor
for all we take in, the tons
of everything we store in stores
and closets, the warehouses
of cookies, panty hose, frozen
juice bars, compact disks, tires
and all manner
of little plastic thing. I cannot
move about the garage stuffed
like a Christmas goose
with rubber grommets, rusty
baling wire, cases
of motor oil, two freezers, big
white sepulchers holding
entrees in waiting, left over
gray-green soup
and an old ham
with freezer bite. We have
two at least
of everything, like an ark
for too much living.

It may well be
a sentimentality, but what of
the cruel farm that made me, one
hammer, one plow, a single
big black horse
to pull it over just enough dirt
to fuel us all, and give us
cake and ice cream too
on Sundays. And a pantry
of pickled pears, corn, cukes, beans
and tomatoes, year in and year out
in the same jars, four neat shelves
filled by October, bare
by July, each jar
holding the taste of summer.

Is being sick
of what I have
maybe a matter
of growing old, a danger
stained by too much time
alone in coffee shops?

Stop me. Shake
me. Bring me back.

THINGS

Here
choked by chickweed
and thistles, guarded
by the noise of crickets
and thwapping grasshoppers, is
a paintless door, to a house
spent. Someone with a title, probably
in a white shirt and tie, has stapled
a yellow paper to the door, a flag
warning busy noses such as mine
that there is danger within, unsafe
boards, unstable ground, rot.

Out here, with
no great use in sight, no
highway planned, no
developments in the works, no
hope, the white shirts have decided
to let physics and termites and
boys with matches
settle the issue, erase
the problem. No
tax money will be spent
to bulldoze down these boards
or raise this house with perfect flames
while men in black slickers and hats
like ducks' bills watch
from their big, red trucks.

I would
torch this tired house myself
if I had the gasoline
and matches and
I was just a little crazier or angrier

'cause this forgotten house
disturbs me.

There's the smell of rust
and spent linoleum and
wet mattresses and pee stains
and old cracked toilets
and canned goods turning to garbage
on shelves clotted with dead bugs and
the must of moths, all manner of
insect cadaver
and spider casts, too.

But more
it is the things
of someone else's living
which goosepimple my flesh, the
impersonal things, the dusty
sewing machine and old cook pot and broken
picture frame and
the can opener
yawning on the wall, the cookie tins
and half empty box
of baking soda and pair
of men's underwear used
it appears
to wipe oil from a dipstick and hung
from a nail in the hall, the things
less important than the something
which tore
the people from this house, a funeral
or a sudden caving-in
of caring, the things
too loaded with meaning
to find burial
in a land fill.

At home, I have a garage
loaded to bursting with such things
and even a rented space
in a queer building alongside
the rented spaces of others
with the same disease, all bursting
with things not yet ready
for the flea market
or the dump
or effort, waiting for a tragedy
to disperse them like seeds
in a forest fire, relatives and friends
come to take their pick
but storing them in a garage or queer building
where they will breed.

Lucky for me
I am afraid of this house
and the house is cabled up
with chains and locks and I'm
much too old to risk the jagged glass
guarding the windows.

AUTOPSIES

Table Three

The subject is an old white male
with no remarkable evidence
of external trauma save for
the lack of eyes. The subject has
unusually long, slender arms
with orbs of tough muscle
at the shoulders. As I open the subject
from sternum to pelvis
a foul odor clouds up, a smell
like meat left three days
in full sun. As I explore the cavity
with my hands, remarkably
I find nothing except a repair manual
for a 1954 John Deer tractor and
a dog-eared Catechism. I should note also
that I cannot find
the subject's rectum. The tongue
is black
and unusually large. When I
open the cranium I find an orange slice
covered with green lint
and when I bisect the small, dust-dry brain
I find the missing rectum
tucked away inside
like a nut.

Table Seven

The subject is an old white female
with blue-veined, slackened breasts
that flow to the knees. There is no hair
on the body and the fingernails
are so long they curve around
the tips of the fingers. There are pieces

of peach peel and what looks like flesh
under the nails. There are signs
of a struggle, bruises on the throat, the breasts
and the thighs. The head is missing, but I find
what looks like brain matter within the pouting
mouth cavity. The vagina, curiously, has been
sewn shut crudely with
a ratty, brown shoelace. When I snip the stitches
air rushes out smelling
of honeysuckle. An internal exam
of the birth canal reveals
that the subject, remarkably, has
13 cervixes sprouting flowers which I think
are ranunculi, bright purple, orange, red
and pink. I also find two brown eyes
which neatly fit the sockets
of the subject on Table Three.

These
are difficult cases. There is
so little clear evidence
to go on. Perhaps they are
someone's parents. It is hard
to know for certain
in this weak light.

THE VAGARIES OF WANT

I want the woman
with the shiny black
hair. She has
curious bright white skin, white
like new bond paper, and I bet
that it's cool
to the touch, and her flesh
October delicious
in that place the dead poets
called the loins.

But she is over there
laughing beautifully at some thing
her male has said, something
I imagine
not nearly as witty
as what my brain shits each minute
as unworthy of voice, and I
am over here, a distance
of twenty-two feet.

I want her
yes
but these days
want her like I want
a dozen black roses, a scoop
of mango sherbet, the neighbor's
new aluminum ladder
or less body hair.

In those days back then
twenty-two feet was a matter
of a single stride, the space between us
a simple matter
of one deep inhalation. Then, then, the want

would burrow in like a badger
and take possession of all those cells
that float like flaming pine needles
at the very ends of nerves.

And it was
very serious business, a transaction
of being.

These days
I am easily moved
by the vagaries of want, the way
it cheerfully goes
as slyly as it comes, never ever
quite loud enough in my ear
to throw me through the air.

HUSSIES

1. Sara Tonan

She performs nightly
naked, without pasties, in a shack
on the other side of my tracks, in
the chemical swamp of my neurons, comes on
to me
like caffeine, supercharges my head
and sends little jolts of juice
prickling down my spine.

She's a looker, she is, no dog-faced whore
who couldn't get office work, but
an artiste, this shack
her *atelier*, all these synapses
her adoring boys. She's got
the tightest, cutest little ass
you've ever seen, and *hello!* breasts
and plump, purple nipples.

She sends
all the boys to heaven
and hell, when they line up
along her stage like monkeys
hoping for a slice of orange
or a nut.

Oh boy!
does she deliver, loving her dance pole
slowly, starting low
on the greased pole, straddling
its chrome shine, her smoking labia made slick
with her whiskied spit, her pussy lips wrapping
'round the pole like tongues. Slowly, like blood
ballooning a stallion's cock, she
unwinds off her haunches

as the music pounds, her pussy lips
fluttering as she rises up, the red and blue lights
electrifying the slick chrome pole
and playing like nasty hands
over the sweet sweaty buns
of beautiful Sara as she slides up
the slippery pole, the monkeys
all the while hooting like coots.

By the time her sparking pussy
has done its work
bolts of hot yellow light
are zinging through every nerve
of the monkey boys.

How does she do that?!

they exclaim, all the while
whistling and sweating and
soiling themselves
and stomping their feet
like petulant children, rocking
sweet Sara's stage and the shack
swaying and every bull frog in the swamp
joining in.

2. Nora Pen Ephron

There's a knock
at the door, a smart, girlish
rata tat tat rap
from a smart dame who knows
what she wants. He can see
her silhouette through
the frosted glass of the door, backlit
by the dim, sputtering bare bulb hanging
in the hall. Even
in silhouette

he can tell she's got
a little, upturned nose and full lips
and a hat
only a dame who's trouble and in trouble
would ever wear, cocked. He brushes
the ashes off his tie, scrapes
at the mustard stain on his vest
and wades through
the stacks of dusty files and wadded-up
sandwich wrappers and Styrofoam cups
to the door.

When he opens the soughing door
sweet trouble
sure enough sweeps in, a knockout body
in a tight, red suit, a shock
of curly black locks
pouring from under the red hat.

    I'm Nora, Mrs. Nora
    Pen Ephron. Are you
    the private dick?

she asks, her big, red eyes
thick with tears, her painted lips
trembling.

    I am

he says, then listens
to the fevered, sordid story
of her straying husband and the tramps moving
in and out of hubby's office
like delivery boys then hears
of her unhappiness
and the strange dreams with wolves and snakes
and the terrible, murderous thoughts.

Ya gotta help me

she sighs, gushing tears
over the full lips, dripping them
off her chin onto his desk.

*Shush. Sure
I will*

he says
as he takes her soft, blubbering body up
in his arms
to comfort her. After a time she sighs
again, kisses his neck and then begins
to suck little guppy sucks
at the loose folds
under his jaw.

But I got no money

the dame whispers
and then gently cups
his balls with both hands.

*He never lets me
have no money*

she says
as she slowly rakes her sharp red nails
up the full, long length
of his hardening member.

Help me

she whispers
then roughly thrusts her salty tongue
down his throat, stirs it around

as if looking
for something in particular.

In one brisk move
he swipes his desk clean
of the papers and the ugly black phone
and the lies
and takes her down
to the cool mahogany, shucks her
like an ear of sweet corn, shucks her
of the red skirt and
the slippery pink teddy, sets loose
her warm, slack titties
which whap at him
as he noshes
on her fruits, wordlessly, careful
he is
not to add to the lies
gathering like bills
in his drawers, noshes
'til the room is searing.

After she is gone
he lounges in his chair and milks
his cigarette, smells her
lingering on his fingers. He feels calm
and oddly complete
in the air of her perfume, their sex
and the cigarette, smiles
and thinks himself
the greatest private dick
to ever roam the mean streets
of this town.

3. Dopa, Mean

When Dopa Meany stormed
into Flora's House of Eggs
all the men
hung their heads, hid
behind forks of food
like elephants behind trees hoping
that Dopa's business
was not theirs, too, while the wives
and girlfriends stiffened their backs
and stared
bug-eyed
at the saucy-bodied tart
in the snug, floral summer dress
which was
of a fabric both slick and shiny
and barely built to contain
her shuddering breasts. But
there was wariness, too, 'cause
Dopa was of two dispositions, one
soft and seductive as silk, the other
mean as a wolverine, just as like
to rip your head clean
from your body as give you
the head action of your dreams, in the back
of your pickup truck or
in the toilet stall
of Joey's Blue Moon Bar. Thus Mean
became the name the fertile boys
and plump, jealous girls came to call
the trashy, fire-tongued girl
with the body god-made to bring
the gruffest, smelly man
down low.

On this day
it was Dopa the Mean

clomping in a sweat to the booth
where the Banks brothers
ate waffles and bacon with Skeet Peterson
and poor Wyman Banks
the man of her mission, making himself small
as Dopa barked like a terrier
inches from his ear
about last night
and this morning
about rudeness and his mama
and promises broken while outside
in the rusting, sky-blue Mustang
her three children fought
over the box of Cheerios, each child
sired by who-knows
under stars, under scratchy blankets
smelling of the breath of beer.

It was kindly Bub Billups
the courthouse custodian
who told
the threadbare story, held the theory
that Dopa was made mean
in the crooked house out
by the old cement plant, made mean
by Papa Meany who Bub says raged
at his young daughter's body with his own
and was known
on one winter night to chase
his screaming, bare-assed daughter
through the snow
made silver by the moon.

QUEEN

After a life of grunting
and sweating, of always being
the weight bearer, the burly *paterfamilias*, a life
of shoveling, sawing and hammering, of always
being the one to carry
the impossibly heavy box, the one
to scare off the prowler, the one
to talk tough to the neighbors, after
thousands of hours of manning the oars
and being the stern muscle at the stern
of the canoe, after all this
on a hot day paddling my family
up the Russian River with no end in sight
only bend after bend of gray water
and blue trees, after too much of something
something snaps
and I stand suddenly up in the canoe
and declare

    enough!

pull
my fleshy, shiftless, nestle-cone son by his scruff
from his pillowed throne in the middle of the boat
and hand him the oar, plop into the vacated throne
stare coldly
at my drop-jawed wife and say

    woman, boy, take me up the river

and stunned, they do, their oars
dipping and dripping, their breaths
struggling against the strange labor
of carrying my weight.

I am Nefertiti, queen, the most desired woman
in all Egypt, gliding down the Nile
on the Royal Barge, just
out for a ride. I hear the rasps of the slaves
as they work to move my magnificence
up the great river, can almost hear
their blood boiling
and smell their sweat
through the haze of my perfume
mingling with the scented oil
oozing from my flesh
and the sweet stench of the fig juice
on my lips and
bejeweled fingers. I am naked, my nipples stirred
by the hot breath of the desert
smoking across the river. The red, blue
and gold silks lap at my body, smooth as a pearl
and plucked hairless just this morning
by the plump hands
of my adoring
Nubian slaves. My loins
are still wet
from his spilled seed, the leavings
of a sweet, hard boy
brought to me
just as I was waking warm
as coddled milk
from the purring of the twin great white tigers
who share my bed. I
am Nefertiti, queen, the most desired woman
in all Egypt.

And I am father, husband
aging man.

CLASS COMES CALLING

There is other evidence
(like my tendency
to eat the rice pilaf
before my entree, my hoarding, and
overeating at potlucks) but
the clearest evidence of my class, clear
as a sunburn says *too long*
in the sun, is my white trashing
of this hotel room: I ate the pillow mint
before my bags arrived
and lied to the bellman
about my lack of change. I called the concierge
to ask his opinion of the local fare
when I know I'll eat at the diner
across the way, all lit up
by screaming pink neon. I'll
swim in the pool
just because I can and take
the pool towel back to my room
to squirrel away in my duffle 'cause
they never count the pool towels. Lounging
with the remote control, the sound
cranked high, I will
pick my nose and mount the boogers
on the lamp shade, maybe even masturbate
and wipe off my belly
with the bedspread. I will
steal the pens and ugly paper
from the desk
and store them never-to-be-used
in a drawer at home. I will shower
until I pucker, hoping, always in vain
to drain the water heater, and flush twice
when I hear my showering neighbor's arietta
through the wall. I will siphon up

the sexy little bottles
of shampoo and lotion, take
the sewing kit, shower cap
and shoeshine mitt, add them
to the basket
overflowing in the garage. I will
order more towels, use each
once, then scum them up
on the floor. When it's dark
I will ride the elevator up
and down, haunt the halls, steal food scraps
and lipsticked wine glasses
from the room service trays
put out from the doors
like cats. I will rise early for the free
continental breakfast, stuff myself and slip
under my shirt
four muffins and an apple
that I will never eat. I will
check out late, but before I go
I will prowl the halls once more
hoping to happen onto
an unguarded housekeeping cart
spilling over with pillow mints and pens.

I've hidden this all
behind my fancy shirt, tie
and the knife-like creases
in my pants. You will not see
dirt under my neat nails. But
this squat women in the pink dress singing
in Spanish as she strips the bed, she knows
the ugly truth of me, knows the things
education cannot hide, about
the cruel crooked house, the
rusting, dead appliances
sprouting from the yard, knows

about the mean black dog
chained to the porch, sees through
the heavy masks
of my airs and erudition.

A DIRTY LITTLE SECRET:

Fair going
pleases me.

1.

At the pig barn, while the herd
of parents in stiff jeans and
the sticky-fingered boys and girls pet
the fuzzy, hours-old piglet, I watch
closely
the designated pig wrangler, a stout 4H girl
in pressed white shirt and pants, a crisp
green scarf 'round her neck. The Fair
is lousy with sturdy, well-fed women
with sun-cooked noses
and red, beefy arms. They all talk
loud
and walk with purpose
like milk cows, udders full, coming in
for relief. They ride horses
fast
across the arena, their bouncing rumps
stacked like potato sacks
atop the rumps of their mounts, their nifty hats
fixed to their bunned-up hair
with pins. They hit their show sheep
with sticks, whistle
loud
and say *Hey!*
with great authority. They
pitch out shitty straw with the boys
and spit and straddle fences
while they talk about
hocks, fetlocks, barrows, boars, gilts
and gross weights. They could each

snap me like a twig
which
excites me very much.

2.

Here
there are warehouses
full of amateur industry, shelves
dripping bright pin cushions and
hand-stitched dolls, quilts
the size of Nevada
labored over all winter by Ethel
and her cackling, blue-haired friends, shelves
of runny peach pies and cookies
stacked just so on paper plates
and competing German chocolate cakes
each missing a wedge, stolen
by a fat judge named Howard. Stunning
are the paintings
struggling to be Elvis or some kid
cradling a gerbil, I think, and splotchy works
of postmodern genius, rendered
by the little people
at Minty White School. I never miss
the photographs, the big slick prints
of barns
and bunches
of green and purple grapes
which nearly scream
to be looked at
and grainy nudes
of someone's willing girlfriend
draped like an old coat
over a sofa, and experiments
gone horribly wrong, all matted
and there on the temporary walls
and all earnest as a tide and wholly

without shame, commentary
or price tags. In this building
the human, making mind
is trotted out
and cucumber marmalade and white fig jam
qualify as art, not food.

3.

On the first day
I move from booth to booth
like the Stations of the Cross
after Polish sausage dogs
with optional grilled onions
and green bell peppers
50 cents extra
dripping grease
and baby-back ribs floating
in a swamp of watery baked beans
and cole slaw
and plastic cups of flat, warm beer
and boats of artichoke hearts
deep fried
in a secret batter and corn dogs
stacked like firewood
under heat lamps and curly fries
so heavy with fat
that they straighten
when you lift them to your mouth and
pudgy, tri-tip sandwiches
served up by ruddy men
from the Lions Club all wearing
the same plaid shirts and white straw hats
and
the trailer trolls, all ashen
and grim, dealing out funnel cakes
dusted with powdered sugar
and piled high with puddles of strawberries

or diced apples bogged down
in a thick goo of corn syrup, all topped
with a fart from the whipped cream can and
at 11 o'clock as they lock the gates I
am in a line of thirty people
for a final fix, for a rubbery cinnamon roll smeared
with cream cheese gunk
and sprinkled
with stale chopped nuts.

It is
a death march, the truest measure
of my emptiness.

4.

On the midway
there are strange, always-skinny men
and women
barking at me, challenging me
to roll a ball
or pitch a dart or dime
and win an ugly, under-stuffed frog or dragon
for the lady on my arm. Sometimes
I take them on
just to be safely close for a while
to these dangerous people
with skin like rhino hide from their days
holding sentry in the sun
at the Ferris Wheel, Fun House
and Tilt-O-Whirl, taking our tickets
into their brown, bony hands
and in a trance of boredom or anger or psychosis
buckling us
into the smelly vinyl seats
for our turns at nausea
and bravado. They live
out beyond the roaring generator trucks

in mobile homes and menace
the shadows beyond the whirring neon, carnies
of the modern era
who no longer know
what *Hey, Rube!* means.

5.

Behold
the fecundity
of The Fair, squirting life out
like blown bubbles everywhere, barnfuls
of the stuff, whole
litters of it: piglets, yes, but also seven
new pygmy goats
and pecking, peeping yellow swarms of chicks
and three new calves with vacant faces
nursing from mama cows
with even emptier faces, and maggots
on the meat scraps in the barrels
behind the Knights of Columbus
barbecue pit. There are
the human signs of fucking, too: screaming kids
running in orbits around pregnant mothers
pushing double-wide strollers and couples
everywhere you look, pubescent
Siamese boy-girl twins, joined
at the hip, the boys' hands boldly jammed
down the pants of their sex sisters, their lips
puffy from hours of kissing
and who knows what else, strutting past
the grinning old men
eating sweet corn.

6.

Where else can you see
human grotesques

like the man with no nose (the nose
eaten, my son guesses, by the sun
or the man's wife in a fight) quietly standing
on the periphery, watching the parade
with his cigarette, smoke billowing
from the holes in his face, like me
come out briefly into the light
to be with his people?

7.

Best yet
there are no rich here, except
the sincerely insincere women, volunteers
wearing jeans which escape their drawers
once each year
to stand timidly at the back
of the Band Boosters Cob Booth
prissily dipping boiled ears into the butter vat
terrified
of all this mucky, swarming, untidy life
which has this week pitched its tent
on the edge of their town.

MAZE

Woman, this house
is too big for my needs. It's a maze
of narrow stairs, stories stacked
upon stories, alcoves, nooks, closets
big as airport hangars, acres
of cold, windowless rooms up
and down
all around and at every turn
there's more: ponderous, elephant-like sofas
and dark mahogany tables
smelling sharply of wood wax and
thick-leafed waxy plants and lamps
with fringed shades and room after room of bad art.

Where   are   you?
I   miss   you.

Are you sewing
in that nameless ugly room
near the top of the top stairs? Napping
in that queer, crooked room that's
three lefts and two rights
I think
from the third floor balcony? Or
are you pooping
in that little dark toilet
I can never find
even in daylight?

I'm hoarse
from calling your name
but hear only
my own thunder and ticking clocks. I'm weary
of climbing stairs, peeping
into black rooms, sniffing

your spent clothes, hunting
the air for the scent of you, tracking you
like a dog.

So, I'll tape this note
with directions and a map to me
to a toilet seat 'cause
you'll have to use it
eventually. But
tape it to which one? There are three
in this house
and one I can't find.

No, better that I sit
fast in this grotesque chair
and hope that you
happen by. I'll lay in wait for you
with a butterfly net.

Those white-shirted social psychologists
are in error on this one: mice in mazes
are not after
the pellet of food, they're trying
to get back to their mice lovers, their
mice pack, their mice people. The mouse
with the fastest time through the maze
is not the smartest mouse, but only
the most lonely.

MACONDO

Overhead
the wind chimes
and the fuchsia bells
stir
while down here
on the lolling red porch swing
nap sleep comes and goes
speaking of Michelangelo
and soft women
I'd forgotten and
clicking blue grass
in a hot brown field
stored for fifty years
in a neuron, a node on the net
thought lost. How it is in naps
in summer
that are not really sleep
and not really dream
but trances
winding like paths in a park
that suddenly stumble upon
what good there might have been
back then
found in the half-not-quite sleep
like dinner mints springing up
in a pocket
of an old coat, and sweet
that way, so that
you bear down hard
to hold on to the nap
even as a car rumbles past
or a plane prattles over. Only here
in this queer fog
do I feel certain women
and see boyhood friends

as they were, hiking up
their corduroy pants
and spitting, and a peacock
on a tin barn roof, and a gray cat
slowly crossing
the snowy dooryard, and a fat black bird
on the bell rope
shaking off the rain. Finally
in middle age
a Macondo summer comes
if even for only
a hundred minutes
instead of a hundred years.

AT THE DOG GROOMER

The clapper bell
on the screen door
jangles as it slaps
against the frame, announcing
me.

The handsome woman
in the rubber apron, Gloria, the one
with the bleached bloodless puckered hands, she
always greets me
with a nod and a smile, frames
every salutation with *Mr.* and *sir*. She always fusses
over my goofy, rat-faced Malamute, scratches the beast
between its ears, tells me
how beautiful she is.

This trip
a poofy-haired, perky woman I recognize
from her pink, toreador pants, is at the counter
chatting with Gloria, holding
a pink leash
connected to a white, fluffy, bread loaf-sized
yipping thing, just made fluffier
and garnished with a bow
that perfectly matches the leash. It takes
all my strength
to keep my dog at bay, keep her
from tearing the ears
off the fluffy thing.

Not too long ago
this scene would have sent me
howling 'til my eyes bled, but
forgive me
now I honor the civility

of this all, the largely harmless message
of leisure
and expendable income.

The clapper bell
on the screen door
jangles as it slaps
against the frame, announcing
me. I am
finally here. The farm boy
still smelling of compost
and bloody chicken feathers
has arrived.

THE BEAST

You tell me
clear and certain
that you have always
thought yourself ugly, tell me
it's a fact
like gravity or death
bored home each day by the beast
you see in the mirror
and visible you say
in the eyes of men.

Your cutting tongue
and dismissing hands
say this, too
throwing sticks on a fire
built and stoked by forces
I never quite understand, but see
each morning I think
as my frowning wife turns
and turns in the mirror, smoothing
this and that with her hands, trying
to will some change
in what she sees.

And it would seem
that the beast leaps from the mirror
and rides with you all day, gnawing
at your insides, hardening
your eyes, making a rod
of your spine. I no longer
try to touch you, fearful
that your edges will cut me.

For what
it's worth: I am

a shallow, petty
and often vain man. I
only give time
to the lovely, precious
and exceptional. You are
all of these. I know
you never kill the beast, best it
with words, but I try here
to be your mirror for a moment
and tell you
that you are beautiful
are beautiful
and each time I find you again
at a table, waiting, and often
in the mirror in my head that never lies
I make of you
what drives me
and most every man
on earth.

MOLT

    for Joseph Stroud

When the talk turns to family
you dart your eyes, turn
skittish, and bolt into the cracks
of our conversation
like a lizard flushed from his sunning spot
on the garden wall, your tail twitching
as you slither into the pauses, the dark
and the cool and the safe
between stone words.

Once, mechanically, you flashed us
a photograph of your brothers
and another of you
standing in front of
some great temple, young
you were, your skin
clear and smooth and taught, hugging you
like shrink wrap. There is pain
here
as you lower your voice and your eyes
and whip through the photographs
like flash cards of multiplication tables or
the unfathomable verbs
of some strange language.

Perhaps like the lizard
your skin has become tired, brittle, slack
and ill-fitting, has grown heavy
with pain. So you tuck away the photographs
and show us, read us, beautiful poems
about this and that, the brothers revealed
in fine layers of words, corium
and epidermis, image
and metaphor, the hurt

sloughing off as you molt, the husk
left on the garden wall for us
to find, collect in cigar boxes
of translucent understanding.

AT THE FRICK

Wife
or no wife, in an elevated moment
I imagine again how to sell myself
to women, that I could sell myself
to women, in particular
to the dark, beautiful woman
lounging like a leopard
in front of the Fragonard.

Madam,

I'd say, perhaps
with a French accent

To save time
let's keep this simple. You
are a beautiful woman

I would say

and I, well, I
à la Symphony in Flesh Color and Pink
have Whistler's soul. Corot felt
what I feel most often. Though I strain
for the clarity of Ingres, most often
what I get
is Greuze, or sometimes David
if I'm lucky. And like Watteau
I'm lighter in the background
than in the foreground, and my life
yearns after the disheveled man
leaning against the arch
and smoking the long-stemmed pipe
in The Portal of Valenciennes. And
to be fully forthcoming

I should probably admit
that for about 24 hours each month
Shiele makes complete sense
and my dream life
is never more complex
than Claude's Charing Cross Bridge
or quite so lovely
as Vincent's
Watermill at Grennep.

What chance
do you think I have, disregarding
for the moment, my lovely wife
tapping her rolled-up catalog
on her arm
as she stares long and hard
at the Holbein?

MELADA

It hasn't all of it
been Calvary. Only
in those dark seconds
when I'm sickly precious as puppies
do I spoil myself with thinking
that my way has been
all thorns
and more than my share
of the lash. Even I laugh
at the vision of me suspended naked
from a rood, my legs
broken, my side
gushing, my lips
dripping vinegar, bad wine.

Because there is you, how
to explain you? Some meed I've earned
for diligence, say, or
perseverance, some little
accidental act or unconscious moment
when I was kind
when I needn't be, noticed
by the gods? If you boil me down
like cane, you are
what's left, a thick resin
of sugar and molasses.

Maybe
I just grew tired
of my own anemia and saw finally
that a living diet
is more than fats, proteins
and complex carbohydrates, that sometimes
the body, even the medulla stuff, needs sugar

in its purest form, needs
surest sweetness.

Before you
I never liked or allowed
candy in my body, but now
downtown
it feels good and right
to hold your hand
and turn into the sweet shop
for a chocolate-covered
strawberry, licorice drop, or
half pound
of peanut brittle. You are
a habit now, a food group
my cells must have.

THE ABUNDANT FLESH OF OTHERS

I have ceased to otherize
most of the most othered, have long since
made mad intellectual peace
with darker skin, same sex sex, and people
without penises, but
forgive me
these massive ovate beings
eating at the next table
are still *over there*
and not me, *outré* they are
and fat, fat, fat
all three of them, wedged
into their chairs, putting great strain
on their shirt seams
and physics generally.

I'm told it's complicated
like Quantum Mechanics as an is is, but
as othering operates I see only mouths
and consumption, sweaty blobs of mushy flesh
panting like dogs in August shade, chowing
through their hillocks of food, feeding themselves
and perhaps too their mothers and fathers
hiding within.

A confession: In the movie house
when I see the big round man moving
like a fog bank to his front row seat, I
quickly look away, but even over the din
of the pre-curtain banter, I can hear
his wheezing, struggling lungs and swear
I can feel the floor tremble
and groan. I'm told by the priests of *other*
that this behemoth
is not otiose, is not maybe

in control of his thermostat or how
his fuel is stored, that genetics
like the shape of my nose has wired him
to pocket away energy like a squirrel
or acorn woodpecker
for a harsh winter
that never comes.

It isn't fair
I know, I'm told, but
I've made such men, this man
in the big blue pants, the poster child
for excess
and wonder
(naively, I'm assured)
what would happen
if he stopped eating, put down
the tub of buttered popcorn
and swore himself off all
but what's stored, wrapped
like bright pink insulation
around his flanks, held himself
to what's squirting out
from under his shirt? How long
would he live
and what's stopping him?

When naked
what does he see
or feel
if even with my 7% pudginess
I turn like a rotisserie in front of the mirror
and pinch myself here, and there, and loathe
what gathers, the folds
between my fingers? What courage he has
I say I guess in a final act of othering
to take a front row seat

with still more food in his hands, a man
without wrists, elbows or a neck, feeding
what emptiness I think I know more
than I wish to tell, but about which finally
I can only guess I guess.

EVERYTHING

To be fully awake, not numb
of mind or hung over by sleep
or dream, to be truly as awake
as a toothache, this
is everything, I think, for only in my
few seconds unclouded by
drink or food or just day weariness
have I seen really seen, really. O
to have all the synapses clicking
and humming, the nerve
from the eye to the brain
firing cold and clear as ice. Then it is
that I am sentient and certain
that there's a job for me in the world
and children are honestly what they are.

Sleep
is the enemy of knowing, no? We
sleep too much and live like dogs
napping by the fire all day, one eye open
here and there, now and then, to check
the food dish, while outside
they are building bridges
without us.

If you ever see me
dozing off, take a taser to my ass
or cuff my ear, hard, and remind me
of what I say
here.

CRICKETS TO THE ANCIENTS

Travelling in late summer
at dusk through the grasslands
I turn off the conditioned air, roll down
the windows in hope
of some nostalgia, a dead smell revived
or some buried image
come welling back like debt. I park
the car, tear my best pants
and a patch of skin on the barbs
as I climb the sagging fence. And
for what?

For this, I think: to walk at dusk
through the recently-baled field
and find this smell
of boiling heat and hay and hear
the crickets come out of hiding
as the air cools, during this time
when there is no pain
and everything works
as it was intended, not
a nostalgia, but a fact that I miss
and will never be able to make the same.

I forget. Tell
me. What did crickets at dusk
mean to the ancients? Tonight
when my old skin, dry
and inflexible as parchment, is in
your young hands, remind me
please
of what they mean, clicking
and singing
as the sun goes down.

BEACH

1.

The path to the beach
is long, steep, rocky and narrow, a gauntlet
of poison oak, head high, slapping out
from both sides, barely
enough room for
a man and his beach chair. I hear her
struggling up the path
from the beach
and already I fear
her fear, what will necessarily come
when we fumble through
our passing.

I stop
and watch her pick her way
toward me
over the stones. I can tell
she's a veteran of this path, nimble, each footfall
efficient, her toned body
always in balance, her broad hat level, something
you could eat from
even as she moves, her eyes
down
consumed by her work.

With a sense women have
evolved out of necessity

    perhaps smell or something
    deeper and more troubling

she knows I am there, parked
in the path. Two strides short of me
she stops, uncoils herself, makes herself

tall
the way certain snakes, birds
and lizards do
when there is danger
and gives me that hard face I've seen before
on streets and from behind steering wheels
and even in the bedroom, her body
rigid and her eyes
welded to mine.

She is beautiful, forty
I'd say, sweating
under her big hat, her chest heaving
from something sadly more
than exertion.

She is slim
and alive. Tenderness bubbles
beneath her stare. She is
desirable.   I say

    hello

much too brightly and
she coils a little, so I dance step
smartly to one side, flatten my body
against the wall of poison oak, carve out for her
a scant nine inches
of buffer, of safe space. She
lowers her eyes, says a soft

    thank you

and not
only to me
as she scrapes by, her damp butt
brushing my leg, passing

a clot of wet sand
from her
to me.

She doesn't
look back. I watch her
until I cannot watch her
anymore.

On the beach I strip, stretch out, take up
a pinch of her wet sand, watch the sun
dry up the little which will ever pass
between us, this good, mostly harmless man and
this rightfully wary woman.

2.

Nestled in the smelly kelp
of the tide line, I find a squatting gull, still
alive, but barely, with just enough blood
and calories left to lift and crane its neck, give off
a goofy grin and squawk

    Look at me.
    I'm gonna die, I'm gonna die, I'm gonna die.

But forgive me, I am
anthropomorphizing
a bird in pain. Always the good son
I crush it
with a driftwood stump.

3.

Two blankets away
a couple is exploding. She
is on her feet, her face wrenched
into something unholy, screaming. He

now
is on his feet
bellowing back. Now
the woman's mouth
is bare inches from his jaw
screeching words that are vacuumed up
by the ocean. Though I can't make out
the words
I can smell the ugly garbage fumes
which fly off the breath of rage, a
familiar smell
which sits in a stratum above the sand
long after the woman
storms from the beach, followed
in minutes
by the hang-dog man.

4.

Eleven, twelve
very young men
and women, prancing like ponies, kicking
up sand around a driftwood fire, drinking
and chucking the crushed cans
into the darkness, laughing
the laughs of bodies
out of control, taught flanks
and perky buttocks, their loins
enflamed
and barely contained
by the spandex
and the silly, hopeless laws
which govern such things.

5.

Clouds
have taken away the moon. I feel my way
up the path on all fours, cut a hand
on a tin can, a glacier
in the clay. I can't see the blood
but I can taste it, spilling out
over everything. There is nothing I can do
but hum
and wait.

YELLOW LIGHT

In such a light
Travis Bickle did his murderous things
in the stairwell, the awful yellow
sucked in along with his rage
from the late-day air outside. In
this dusky yellow light
promises are made and children
see God walking and all women
are beautiful, all men
desirable. Moths live
and flutter within
such light, yellow moths
with nothing to do
but live in the buffered spaces
between the molecules
of dying day. The body
is washed of pain
and the eyes sharpen
in the yellow light thrown off
by the sun, spent, its white light
muted by the fatigue
off all day working
to make shadows.

This yellow light is perfect
and selective, like a hand moving
through peaches in a basket, squeezing
each, deciding the best
for the eyes to eat, a yellow
rich and almost palpable, the feel
of gold feathers rolling over
against your skin.

In this light
the boy touches himself

and the girl touches herself
and both come to know
that all things delicious and dangerous
arc and spark this time of day
in yellow light, including metaphor
and the trope of the sun
made flesh.

SO IT BEGINS

I see all this
in fragments
through the balloons
and the sea of sweet-smelling bodies
from my roost
behind the cookie
and lemonade table:

After an hour
of bouncing, frenzied skipping
and sweating to drums and electric guitars
the music suddenly slows
and some urgent, girly voice
begins to sing silly
about "my man." My son
edges over to the patch
of impossibly slim, flushed girls, edges over
to the tallest and god bless him
most comely of the lot
and mumbles something (I can see
his sweaty lips moving) and
without a word from her
but maybe earlier
through an intermediary or
some gesture I've long since ceased
to read or understand, she goes with him
out into the hot empty middle
of the great linoleum plane
where he locks his
wet pudgy fingers
into the spindles of her hands
and they begin to move, more
a slow rocking in place
than a dance, their eyes
closed.

So it begins
for him, too, this
cruel, needy dancing. Good luck
boy. Be better at it
than your father. When the music stops
be sure to bow and thank her, and
don't make promises you know
you will never keep, even
in your daydreams.

THE LESSONS OF HER BODY

The First

Toes, napes, bellies, backs
and that scallop of heaven
where the hip begins
its trip to the thigh: Yes, this
is another fragmentation
of woman, but this time
the pieces are what's left
after you've taken the boy
finally
out of the hands and eyes
of the man, finally divested yourself
of your boyish fixations
on pert breasts, nipples
the size of your thumbs, red
mouths, and long legs, long and thin
as ostrich legs, finally gone wisely cold
to obsessions with snug, silken pussies, hair
down to here, and firm little butts
which are really
the butts of boys.

What you come to
finally, joyfully, thankfully
is that numbness after a nap
where you see everything clearly
and it comes to you like influenza
that all women are arousing
and not only
in the dark under the covers
after their bodies have been warmed
and your cool, happy hands
have played over their planes, peaks
and valleys, but even
in the glaring light of day

on a blanket
under a tree where
with the naked eye you can see
finally
that she's all over lovely
and maybe most
between her toes
or in the glowing wisps of hair
stirring on her neck's nape
or in the spongy plot of belly
that deepens her navel.

I could
go on, but I've made
my point, or
more accurately, my wish
that I come
finally
to that place
promised by the great, gristled ones
who claim
that with patience and practice
you can be stirred priapic
by her hair in the tub, or the smell
of her towel, and finally
by the space you sense somehow
she has just left
or is about
to enter.

The Second

Young women
are so blisteringly stupid
about men. Tell me, anthropologically
speaking, has there
ever been a young male
that didn't leave, even

while still in the room? (And a man
that hasn't left
is a coward
or a liar.) Any man
worth his salt
can reason that any woman
is beautiful in the dark
with her clothes shed. (No wonder
our children
are all gimpy, rickets-ridden
things.) Your only hope
woman
is to find some mother-beaten
death-of-a-man so damaged
that he flies home each night
like a skittery pigeon. If you must
hold one close, better
finally
to make yourself rich while waiting for
some brittle-boned rooster like me, all
fucked out
and madly ready
to squire your toes, belly
and the hollow in space
where your body once stood.

A BOX OF CANDY FOR THE AGE OF GOD

It is with sadness that I report
that my pubescent son, still fuzz-faced
and hammy-fleshed from too long
in the womb, has already reduced
the motivation of the world
to "those four square inches"
of wild hair and mucous membrane
so terribly packed with nerve ends
all connected to the brain
in that joyously sinister way.

o

I'm the youngest
of the four leather men
sitting at the lunch counter
without so much as a grunt
or whisper
between us, all effort made
to make our eating spheres
as small as possible, drawn
so far into ourselves, into
our sausages, jam
and runny eggs, that
after a while
even the waitress
ignores us. I watch them
like an owl watches ripples
in the saw grass. I'm learning
how to be old
and male.

o

In sex I am stupid, taken away
so easily by nakedness
and that toxic vapor you cannot smell.

o

Another new virus come to us
from some chance meeting in China
of a feverish chicken
and an off-his-feed pig. This one
is nasty, can cut you down
in a matter of hours. You have to admire
an organism so efficient, so
wholly unburdened
by ethics and such. Welcome
virus H5N1. I wish
you well.

o

A single barking dog
in the deadest hour
of the coldest night
of winter. Its bark
bounces off the snow
and travels miles in echoes
all the way to here. What
do you want? If you are
as lonely as I am, I
can help you.

o

When I go
it will be spectacular. Pieces of me
will arc and crackle, shoot off into oblivion
like sparks from a campfire. When I go
take your children into the street
to watch.

o

Deborah Norville
is on my mind. Years ago
she was on morning television
speaking the news. I try to replace her

with a line of poetry, but
it is no use. So I give her
a terminal disease
and as I stroke her hair
she dies peacefully in my arms.

o

I confess: I murdered
two hummingbirds. It was murder
in the second degree, execution
by neglect, going away
for two weeks, but leaving
their feeder dry in this fallow time
before the first wildflowers. I see them
in a panicked zipping about
until the last calories burn away
and on some bony twig
the final torpor takes hold. There are
many acts for which I've earned its fire, but
it is for these murders that I deserve
the most blistering hole in hell
as the greatest ill
is to make something need you
then pull away like some parlor trick
with candelabra and a table cloth.

o

All mythology considered
saying *FUCK OFF!* to a noisy raven
is temerity defined.

o

I have trained myself
to take sentiment
by the throat and choke it
'til it goes blue in the face, then
after I'm sure it's dead, cut its head off
and shove it up its own ass. But

what to do with this scent
of wild roses mysteriously
in the air
and the white, fine hands of Dorothy
and the click of pruning shears
it conjures?

o

The little girl
is stooped over
an old, sleeping dog, lifting
its tail
and poking at its asshole
with a broom straw. Her
older brother sees me seeing
and slaps her hand. Another intelligence
learns shame.

o

These three very old men
limping by my perch on the park bench
are not going gently, bent
at the waist, guffawing like gut-shot hyenas
and pointing
at my purple shoes.

o

This gnarled black oak
glazed with cold rain in grayest November
is what I had hoped for myself. It is
the fiction I choose, that
and the utility
of the gumbo-limbo.

o

It started small, fluttering
a corner of the table cloth, then moved
across the room to stir the dried flowers

~ 153 ~

on top of the chifforobe, amped itself up
to a thieving of the pilot light, and now
there's a full-fledged wind
in the house, blowing me
into sleep.

o

The most desperate act in the world
is that photograph you take
at the overlook
of the great blue and green
unphotographable panorama, the optical
smooshing of all that grand visual life
into a 3x5 flatness more empty even
than the emptiness
that tripped the shutter.

o

The woman in the beaver coat
and brown satin pants is trying
I guess
to go skin two better.

o

On the other side of this door
is my son, sleeping
in a darkness so thick
that no light known
could ever illuminate him
sleeping there, peacefully, oblivious
to the coal-eyed gorgons under his bed
and the hissing monsters coiled
and waiting for him
beyond his window. I hope
he'll understand
my lie.

o

Wiser, I no longer think
that being inside you
is as close to you
as I can manage. This
residue of toothpaste scum
in the sink, the black hair
glued to the soap bar, the sweet stink
you leave in the air, these artifacts
in truth
are the case I build to prove
that I
am not alone.

o

There's a fat, white worm
riding along
on my coat sleeve. It's all
mouth parts
and digestive system, a
coolly-efficient, perfect
thing. I remember
the bright white swarms of them
writhing within the calf's carcass
and nesting in the half-eaten
blue racer, and suddenly
I don't feel so good
even in my new blue suit.

I name it Snow White, remove it
gently from my sleeve, kiss her
sweetly goodbye
for now.

A HUNGER

In a clot we move, us four
in the night in the cold, away
from the theatre, the film
about a laughing-eyed
serial killer
who made a costume
from women's skins.

We burble about this-and-that
as we stroll
distracted past the yellow-windowed shops
of hats and pastries and toys, past
the stinking steam of coffee shops, past
the colorful mannequins of the dress shop
and the gleaming hardware store.

We stop
unrehearsed
at the white-bright window
of the bookshop and
without discussion
we go in where
our clot disperses, each of us peeling
silently and bravely away
from the pack into the stacks, peeling away
like jets from a tight formation, string
unraveling, like shrapnel breaking
through the body, each fragment finding
its own feeding place.

The mind is bruised
and empty
and it's ravenous.

OPPOSABLE THUMBS

Every morning
I pass by this house
at 1247 Summerhill Road, slowly
hoping to catch sight
of the architect and builder
of the forty-seven sputtering windmills
scattered about the yard. I like
the one with the little man
chopping wood, driven
by some clever mechanism
driven by the propeller
driven by the wind. They are all
brightly painted, mostly
in yellow, red, blue
and green. If it's not cold
I roll down the window
to hear them clacking, clanging
and whirring, and wonder
after the impulse
of setting down bricks
in some order, especially
that risky first one
that leads to the others, to
gleaming hospitals, to death camp
crematoriums.

I don't think
the anthropologists are clear
on the why of this.

Under yellow lamplight
my wife
is making a pillow, my son
is drawing.

THE PLUM IN MY POCKET

represents
sweetest desire. As I
walk the beach through the fog
I can feel it burning there. With
every jarring footfall
it bobs up dangerously
in my pocket, a whisker
from being spit out of my pocket
and into the tide wash.

It would be a great loss
to lose this plum now, within sight
as I am
of the bench where I plan
to sit, give into the desire, cease
being the Catholic boy, and consume it.

But first
I'll fiddle with it, roll it over
and again
in my palm, run a finger slowly
along its butt crack, wipe gently away
that odd, frost-like dust
that patches
the skin of plums. I intend
to enter the plum not
with my teeth, but
with my thumb, enter through
the stem end, that twat dimple
that has forever been the fascination
of boys. When I enter
it will tear north and south
and there will be
an electric start
and a shudder of my shoulders

as I push through its coldness
to its pit.

It will be gone
in four bites, maybe five, and after
I study a minute
the oval stone of its core, I will
flick it from my palm into the sand
and wonder
what the big deal was
and what time it is, how long
'til dinner—*boiled leeks*
and potatoes
with butter and salt—wonder
how long
until I hear her voice from the dark stairwell
calling me to bed.

THE MEAT OF A ROOSTER
IS TOO TOUGH TO EAT

I don't care
if I'm the oldest bird
here, I'm dancing. Got on
my tight jeans and
a sleeveless shirt, looking good
I imagine after a cocktail
prancing
and frothing around
with the best of them, scaring
the bejeezus
out of my foxy wife
and drawing damp stares
from the
heroin-chiced young women, snickers
from the wasted, beer-gutted, dead-lidded boys
prowling the margins
of the dance floor.

Stand
the hell back. I'm dancing
to a brassy band
called Super Booty, and I'm
hanging on to it all, every
second of it, for dear life.

DEAD MAN FUCKING

In the middle of
a languid, loving stroke
I glance left and catch
my reflection in the water glass
on your nightstand, the optics
of water and glass
conspiring like a funhouse mirror
to bend me into something
cadaveresque, a wasting animal
all skin and bones, like some
bagged-out, has-been alpha lizard bobbing
and weaving, displaying
what's pathetically left of himself
in the sun of your body.

It occurs to me
like rain to a dog
that there will be a last time
for this sweet enterprise
that has eaten such
a disproportionately large
slice of the pie, that right now
there are maybe thousands of us
from Reykjavik to Christchurch
grinding away in huts, houses or hotels
in a final go at it.

Infirmity creeps over you
like the last plague over Egypt, slips in
and reduces you
to a mawkish spectator, or
rudely and unceremoniously
cuts you down
like a scrub oak
in the way of a new road.

So
I'll take my time with it, with you
this time, and when we're spent
I'll stay in you
as long as you'll have me and
in the first seconds of sleep
invite amnesia, the loss
of the terrible truth I see
staring back at me
from the water glass.

THE HOWLING SPOT

My perfect wife
isn't quite, the way a gardenia
with one browning petal
is still beautiful
and perhaps perfect only then
because the turning petal reminds us
that the blossom is only beautiful
because the potential for rot
is always out there
lurking beyond the brilliant whiteness
and the perfume. She sees
her browning petal
to be her toes, crooked
as hockey sticks, a genetic thing
that marks her mother
and grandmama. I give her toes
a long look, laugh
and agree, keep from her
the truth, that her true blemish
runs deeper: she never touches me
in the night, you see. A sound sleeper
she curls up with her body
and her dreams, her eyelids
jerking about like kites
as she cycles through
the selfish stages
of her sleep. A dozen times each night
I cup her body in mine
or brush her belly or breasts
oh so just so gently
with the back of my hand. But never once
in our separated hours
does she sigh, unfold an arm
and hunt for me
in that new-moon-night dark cave

which is the nest
of mating. How
can she sleep? Can't she hear
the howling
my skin is making, loudest
the animal yowl coming
from that gangrenous gash
at the base of my spine?

ECTOPIA

Long before men wore shirts
and women wore
flowered dresses, before lips
formed words and long before text
there was a black-haired, beautiful woman
of thirteen years, abandoned naked
by her own kind
under a tree. It is deepest night
and she is shivering
while clutching with both hands
a burning knot in her belly. As she
doubles up, pulls her knees to her chest
in pain, she finds
through the swimming leaves of the tree
stars
and small roaming clouds
lit up by a moon she cannot find
in the night sky. Strange birds
look down on her from their night roosts
in the tree. She does not know
except with a keen shadow of herself
what the pain is.   (She knows only
a different pain, remembers only
the footfalls of her people
walking away from her, building her
no fire, and the tall male looking briefly
her way
before disappearing
into the night)   Something
bursts deep within her belly. Her last
articulation of pain
is beautifully formed, the birthing
not of flesh

but of a word, her lips and tongue, the hollow
of her throat, all singing
a gift
which is echoing still.

THE DEER AT THREE A.M.

Hello, 911? This
is Joseph and I
need help at
405 Senda Ladera Lane. Could you
please send someone quick
to scare the horrible deer away?

They're right outside
eating their way
into the house, their big eyes, big
as big no bigger
than four times cows' eyes
watching me through the windows.

I can hear
their terrible chewing, the plants being ripped
from the dirt.

Bring a big gun and lots of bullets or
better yet stakes
for their hearts.

Come quick. I can
hear them breathing
all around me.

HIGH STREET

Those fiction writers
in the *New Yorker,* so
painfully untidy in their bodies
in story after tiresome story
make it out as
so impossibly complicated, stew
it, render it like a dead horse
into soap, into shades
of the bleakest pathology. But
has it ever been for anyone
more complicated than those first days
on High Street so rightly named, two sets
of hands, legs and lips, a couple
split off from the pack like wolves
paired by a smell or a deep-eyed look
split off to pirate themselves away
to a cave, a small rented room, candles
flaming, and a bed
stinking of the sweet wet act
of seeing if it fits?

And fit it did, over
and over as the sun
ran its cycle out there
behind the drawn shades, again
and again 'til we'd pushed
from boredom against the taboo
and the fit was so snug
that I could no longer feel
you from me. Has it truly ever been
more complicated
than this?

And
for a fortunate few
like us
it fits beyond minutes into years
and the hothouse moments
are punctuated constantly
by kindnesses exclaimed! in an awful fever
even from the darkest corners of the cave.

MAINTAINING THE ORGANISM

On the day the word came
that one of those blood bugs
that terrorize the young
had finally taken
little Aaron Gould, Mrs. Riordan's
third grade class wrote down the names
of all the little things
that can kill you. Rachel Smits
told the story
of Mrs. Lunkel, a
family friend who pricked herself
while sewing, died later
after the tiny puncture
festered. Ronnie Wright's Aunt Lolo
was bitten by a squirrel
in Yellowstone, caught the plague
and perished
after six straight days
of sweating, moaning
and throwing up.

All day
she wrote them down
until the blackboard spilled over
onto six-foot sheets
of butcher paper. When the bell rang
Mrs. Riordan and her little people
filed out
sober as old nuns.

I honor
that you made it somehow
to here, thank you
for spending your precious seconds
on this poem. But maybe it's time

that you wrote your own
or took a walk. Maintaining
the organism
is such hard work
and surprise of surprises
ends so badly, I think.

UNDERBELLY

Like a closet cross-dresser
stealing a peek at himself
in his wife's pink panties, I steal out
of the hotel room while
my wife and son sleep
to study the underbelly
of the city. My wife and son
would tremble in their dreams
if they knew
that it's on these dawn walks
that I'm happy, and maybe
only then, prowling
the alleys and
looking into the dumpsters and talking shit
with the red-skinned folk
groggy in the doorways and stairwells
of the boarded-up buildings. I see myself
in the sooty, cracked glass
of the dead store fronts
and wonder what gene
wormed its way into the daisy chain
of my DNA that explains
why I whistle on these walks
and feel an ease in my gait
among the broken bodies and stench
of these sad, brown-bricked blocks
of uneven sidewalks
and ridiculously skinny cats.

Would I be so joyed
without the fifty in my pocket
and the soft wife and bright son
back there to go back to
sleeping

and the bright green car sleeping
in the hotel's underground garage?

And the answer
frightens me.

BEFORE THE DOORS OPEN

In the very early morning
before even the birds
or the paper boys are about, the windows
of the corner restaurant are set
rattling with music. It's a party
of two Spanish-speaking men
and a woman, mopping floors
and wiping down tables
to the squawk of accordions and organs and
the bleat of trumpets, all punctuated
by a big clear voice
clearly in love
with someone, somewhere. The men
joke I think
with the woman, though it is hard to see
through the steam on the rattling windows and hear
through the strange, joyful music, and even
if I could hear
I wouldn't fully understand.

Later
when the doors open
I slip in for my coffee, hear sadly only
poor worried Mozart spilling
from the speakers, while tucked out of sight back there
among the noise of pots and pans and the deep-fat fryer
the party goes on
without me, without the music, or
any of us all.

THE DIFFERENCE:

I am walking
my son to school. He is
laughing, telling me last night's dream:

he's flying high above
a dazzling, white ocean cluttered
with small, jade-green islands. Suddenly
he loses his ability to fly and plunges
like a sputtering plane
toward an island. He lands
laughing
in the soft white belly fur
of his dog. He flies again
and again, falls to earth again
and again, landing each time
in the thick, warm fur
of the dog.

He asks me
if I remember my dreams. I touch the last
of the white-blond baby down
on the back of his neck
and lie, choke back
the telling of my dream:

I
and everyone I've ever loved
is naked and chained
to a stone wall. There is
a violent storm. The air
is wet and hot. A fat man
in a black hood
is moving from love to love
with an axe, hacking off their legs
above the knee. There is black blood

everywhere
and screaming. Now
it's my turn. Before the first swing
of the axe
the sweaty, fat man
lifts his hood enough
to spit into my mouth. My legs
are pruned from me. The pain
wakens me.

It's a clear
and simple difference
really. My father never
walked me to school or
touched me sweetly like this
on the neck. Instead, my skin
became a bag
for carrying my broken bones
and what I remember most is the smell
of disinfectant, the horrible bright lights
and the rustling stiff white starchiness
of the women
swirling about the blazing room.

My son
will have no need
of poetry, which is a sadness
I can bear.

About The Author

Joseph Keller McNeilly was born in 1949 in LaGrange, Indiana. Across the first twenty-seven years of his life he was shaped by the rural poverty of his family and his connections to the Amish communities of Northern Indiana and Southern Michigan. In 1976 he took his first plane trip, to Vancouver, B.C., to study writing at the University of British Columbia. Since 1978 Joseph has lived primarily in Santa Cruz County, California. He welcomes electronic mail at *jomcneil@cabrillo.cc.ca.us*.

About The Publisher

Chatoyant is a small press on the Central Coast of California publishing short run poetry and art books. Forthcoming books are *And Today I Am Happy*, poems by Penny Cagan and *AEK: The Paintings and Poetry of Anne Krosby*. Contact Chatoyant or purchase our books through our website, www.chatoyant.com.

cha•toy•ant (shuh-TOY-uhnt) adj. Having a changeable luster. From French, present participle of *chatoyer*, to shimmer like a cat's eyes.

About The Type

Out Here was set in Berling. Berling was created by Karl-Erik Forsberg for the Berling foundry in 1951, with other weights added in 1958.